Best wishes for taming your Beast!
Byron G. Sabol

TAMING THE BEAST

SUCCESS WITH DIFFICULT PEOPLE

By

Byron G. Sabol

TAMING THE BEAST: SUCCESS WITH DIFFICULT
PEOPLE

ByeCap Press
9541 Lavill Lane
Suite 105
Orlando, FL 34786

ISBN: 978-0-6151-5840-2

Copyright © 2007 Byron G. Sabol

All rights reserved. No part of this book may be reproduced or transmitted in any form or by any means, electronic or mechanical, including photocopying, recording or by any information storage and retrieval system, without the written permission from the author.

Dedication

I heard from a noble source – the chaplain for the Seton Hall University's men's basketball team – that the two most important days of your life are the day you were born and the day you figured out why. While I was probably not born to author books, I believe I have figured out why I am here: to experience all the greatness of living each day with the two individuals to whom this book is dedicated – my wife, Joy, and our beautiful daughter, Kathleen.

Having been married to me for 30 years, Joy could have easily written this book. Her uplifting spirit is a daily reminder of how the power of a great attitude can work wonders with a difficult person.

Kathleen is my inspiration. She fills each day of my life with all the reasons I need to understand why I am here on earth.

CONTENTS

Acknowledgements

Prologue	i
Chapter 1 – "You Won't Be Here Six Months!"	1
Chapter 2 – Conflict in the Workplace	11
Chapter 3 – Understanding The Difficult Personality	27
Chapter 4 – Are You Sure It's The Other Guy?	33
Chapter 5 – Taking Personal Communications To The Next Level	41
Chapter 6 – Building The All-Important Rapport	79
Chapter 7 – Eight Activities To Improve Personal Relations	87
Chapter 8 – Coping With The Difficult Boss	97
Chapter 9 – Coping With The Difficult Co-Worker	125
Chapter 10 – Coping With The Super Aggressive	135
Chapter 11 – Coping With The Silent Type	143
Chapter 12 – You Are The Solution	149
Notes	153

Acknowledgements

No one I know authors a book without assistance from others. This book is no exception. My heartfelt thanks go to Phyllis Lupo for her administrative support, to Adrian Bland, Thomas Brennan, Daniel Dana, Ph.D., Phyllis Diller, John Ford, David Alan Gibb, Ron Goetzel, Jim Ireland, Karen Jagatic, Loraleigh Keashly, David Lipsky, Steven Loranger, Denise McCabe, Paul Mok, Ph.D., Sue Mosebar, Kenneth Nowack, Ph.D., Rev. Father George O'Brien, Ph.D., Jerilyn Oltman, Karen Plunkett, Christine Porath, Paul Rosch, M.D., Dennis Signorovitch, Lynne Tan, M.D., and Jane Toombs for their valued input.

Authors are supposed to be capable of crafting words that succinctly convey their intended message. I am unable to do that when it comes to acknowledging the immeasurable positive impact my Mother and my Father have had on my life. Growing up in small towns in Illinois, which this book references, was made all the more meaningful because of my family. A special thanks for being there go to my sisters Sharon and Bernadette and to my late brother, Tommy.

Byron G. Sabol

Prologue

Nearly everyone I know – from first grade through highly successful careers in business, industry, and non-profit – has had to communicate and deal with some challenging personalities. Many of these individuals probably believe that the challenges they faced were so unique that no one on the planet had any experience of such staggering magnitude. I really doubt that they had anything on me. Let me explain.

I met my first difficult person early in my life. I was four years old (going on 19) when I smoked my first cigarette. As I sat on the front steps of my Daddy's tavern in Streator, Illinois, I eagle-eyed the 7-Up deliveryman flipping his cigarette towards my direction as if to say "come and get it." What was I to do? I had no choice. I went for it. Those first few drags on that cigarette I picked up off the ground made a man out of me. Four years old and I was in control of my own destiny. That was until the 7-Up man squealed on me and my Daddy came out and kicked my behind. This was my first encounter with a challenging personality – the 7-Up man. I refuse to drink 7-Up!

At the age of six I became the youngest altar boy in the history of St. Patrick's Parish in Minonk, Illinois. Never heard of Minonk? No problem. Few have. It's located between Chicago and Peoria and had, at the time, a population of 2,000 sans dogs, cats, hobos, and cows. I was not chosen to serve Mass in the first grade – most boys didn't start until the second grade – because of some self-defining spiritual powers. No, my family lived about 200 feet from the front door to St. Pat's Church and School, my Mother went to Mass everyday and my sister, Sharon, was the organist. The good nuns weren't stupid. When you have a resource so close, take advantage of it.

Now one of the resources I am referring to was not my extensive knowledge of Latin. You see my Daddy owned a tavern (sound familiar?) – The Glass Bar. As the nip in the fall air arrived, I would be asked by one of the nuns if my Daddy had anything that might help alleviate the pending colds that they were certain would soon befall them. Let's hear it for Barclay's Bourbon! The "nip" in the air interestingly coincided with the "nip" that would soon become available to these dedicated teachers. With certain regularity I was delivering a fifth of "cold remedy" to the rectory for the good nuns at St. Pat's.

In spite of my very *cordia*l relations with several of the good sisters, I found myself facing a real personality challenge as I entered the 6th grade – Sister Mary Herman Joseph. Her name – Herman Joseph – was enough to send cold chills down the backs of mere mortals. She was, as was every nun who taught at St. Pat's, a very devote and hard working soul. There were times, however, when she may have taken her devotion a little too far. You see, she loved to hand out "triple problems" when kids acted up. Don't get me wrong, the kids who were on the receiving ends of these dreaded things usually deserved them. In fact, I believe I tied with Josh Brown to lead the class in triple problem reception. Josh had a bit of an advantage and a disadvantage in his claim to the title. His advantage was that he was three years older than anyone else in the class. His disadvantage is that he was three years older than anyone in the class. All of us were 12 years old and Josh was 15. You see Josh had fallen out of a hayloft on his head and was never quite the same.

Triple problems were a math challenge and if you were not a math wiz, and that included me, you could spend a lot of time working on those blasted things. We usually had to do them instead of going to recess, which added to the pain. If you didn't finish them during recess, you got a bonus – you got to take them home and finish them by the next school day.

Getting help at my house to solve the triple problems I was amassing was like executing a triple play in baseball – highly unlikely. My father never finished the fourth grade and English was his second language. I loved my Daddy, but he was no help. My mother finished an equivalent to high school, and I loved my Mother, but she was far from a math major. In spite of familial shortcomings, the triple problems got done and Sister Herman Joseph took early retirement. Thank the Lord for big favors!

Any experience I would have with triple problems paled in comparison to some of the other challenges at St. Pat's. Take Allan Johnson for example. Following the noon lunch break one day, kids in the 7th and 8th grade were back at their desks ready for the afternoon studies to begin when good Sister looked around and noticed that Allan was not among those in the classroom. You see, several of the 7th and 8th grade boys maintained a less than favorable relationship with Allan. When Sister went outside looking for Allan, she found him on the playground. Not all that bad of a place to be, except that Allan was not playing. Allan was staked out on his back staring up at the sun as it beat down on him like an oven with an open door. Sister untied him, pulled up the stakes, and Allan reclaimed his rightful place in the classroom.

While staking out a fellow student was not a tradition at St. Pat's, initiation for younger boys was. If you were a boy at St. Pat's somewhere between say, the 3rd grade and the 6th grade, you were in for some annual rude treatment. In the fall, we boys had to stand against a wooden fence while the older boys threw not ripened, soft pears – no, that would be too kind. They threw those hard green ones that resembled hand grenades when they hit you.

Prologue

The pear beatings we took were only surpassed by the ice balls that were fired at us each winter as we were lined up against that same dreaded fence. Normal snowballs would not do. Some of those young Nazis placed snowballs overnight in their family's freezer and used them against us. I wasn't even out of grade school and I was accumulating an inventory of experience dealing with some difficult people.

I thought my experiences with difficult people in the classroom were over when I left St. Pat's. Another experience would raise its ugly head – this time in college. On the first day of my Business Law class in undergraduate school, the instructor walked into the classroom and introduced himself saying, "My name is William Eckert. I tried to make it as a lawyer in Detroit and I couldn't, so I decided to teach." Upon hearing this I thought to myself that he is either one of the more honest and forthright teachers I will have encountered or he is just not quite the brightest star in the galaxy. The answer would come in the final quarter that year.

During the first two quarters I received a letter grade of "B" in this class. It was now time for a Sabol full-court press to earn an "A" during the final quarter of Business Law with William Eckert. Two-thirds of the way through the quarter I am rolling. Two exams: Two "A"s for Sabol. Only the final exam to go. During class one day Mr. Eckert was making a point that I did not understand. I turned to the student on my left and asked him if he understood the point and he said no. I then asked the fellow on my right – he had been in the Navy and was married so I assumed he was all the wiser. The ex-Navy guy didn't have a clue. I raised my hand and politely said to Mr. Eckert that some of us did not understand the point he was making and would he kindly explain it further. I had barely finished my request when Mr. Eckert said, "Sabol, I want to see you after class." As class ended I went to Mr. Eckert who said loudly enough for half of the student body to hear: "Sabol, I used to think you were pretty sharp. Now I know better. That was the stupidest question I have ever heard." That was not the kind of comment that bolsters the confidence of someone going on to graduate school. However, I had confidence that Mr. Eckert would treat my work on the final exam objectively and honestly. I was wrong. Although I did well on the final exam, Mr. Eckert gave me an "F". On the postcard that I had left for my final grade to be mailed to me, Mr. Eckert gave me a "D" minus. The university does not give out minuses on final grades. Mr. Eckert did all he could to take my grade as low as possible. That was my last quarter in undergraduate school. I was on my way to California to begin work on my MBA. Mr. Eckert – the man who couldn't make it as a lawyer in Detroit – couldn't make it as a college teacher either. He was fired six months later.

Prologue

Communicating and dealing with difficult people is a formidable task. I hope you find – in the chapters that follow – value to your everyday life. As we begin this journey together, allow me to emphasize the admiration I retain to this day for those called to religious life and who teach our youth. The Catholic nuns at St. Pat's were terrific ladies and devoted educators. Mr. Eckert could have learned a great deal about teaching and about treating others with respect from the good sisters at St. Pat's. But I have something special to be thankful for. If it had not been for those blasted triple problems during the sixth grade and my experience with Mr. Eckert in college, I probably wouldn't have written this book.

Each of these experiences left an indelible mark on my psychic and, sometimes, my body. However, a more compelling experience with a difficult person was yet to come.

Chapter 1 – "You Won't Be Here Six Months!"

> *"Call for help now!"*
> Detective Jack Cates
> *48 Hours* (1982)

The sun was bright and the smog was light on that beautiful mid-1970's fall day in Central California as I rolled along Highway 99 in my Chevrolet Camero from Los Angeles to Visalia reflecting on my career. Visalia is located between Bakersfield, California, made famous for people getting dead as in the movie *The Killing Fields*, and Fresno, California, noted for great raisins, beautiful citrus and not much of anything else. [Author's note: I don't expect this book to be a big seller in Fresno!]

At this time Visalia had a population a little under 40,000 and remains to this day a focus of California agriculture. It is also one of the most attractive and comfortable cities I have ever visited. Visalia was the Northern Division office for Southern California Edison, my employer. I would work that day with the Company's Northern Division speaker's bureau training them on the speech arts.

I was a young tiger at a large electric utility company, one of a handful of *up-and-comers* who played a role in creating one of the preeminent personal communications capabilities of any US-based company. I was a moderately polished speaker and I regularly gave presentations explaining electric utility economics, alternative sources of energy, and nuclear power as a safe source of energy. I knew my career was on the right path, that my future with Southern California Edison held no bounds. Just the day before, I had given a speech in Palm Desert, California. I spent the night in a motel where each room came equipped with its own fly swatter! Alas, my career was on the threshold of greatness.

I had debated environmentalists and anti-nuclear foes on radio and on TV throughout Southern California. The work was exciting and it was emotional at times. Not every audience was there to embrace the utility industry position on growth and the environment. A few of the audiences – especially those on college campuses – were down right hostile. All and all the experience was personally rewarding. But the hue and cry of the anti-nuclear movement was starting to abate. The rush from taking on an adversary on TV, radio, or in front of an energized audience was no longer there. So as I trekked along Interstate 99, following my fly swatter experience, I realized I had a problem. When the only excitement of your job is whether or not you'll make the 240-mile trip from Los Angeles to Visalia on a full tank of gas, you know you have a problem.

I knew it was time to seek other career opportunities. And sure enough, an attractive opportunity presented itself. I became one of 33 original candidates for the position of senior executive for P.I.P.E. (Plumbing Industry Progress & Education), the largest promotional fund for the unionized mechanical construction trades industry in North America. Promoting plumbers may not have been my idea of eternal bliss, but the position I was competing for would challenge my marketing, communications, public relations, and management skills. It was just what I wanted at the time. But I'm sure that's how the other candidates also felt. Soon the number of candidates was reduced from thirty-three to six and I was one of the six. Each of us was interviewed by six of the seven industry principals – one of the seven chose not to participate. No one said why he didn't participate. I didn't ask. I would learn a very simple, all-important lesson: Ask!

After completing my work that day in the Edison Visalia office, I checked my phone messages to learn I had been selected over the other candidates for this new position. What a euphoric feeling. Was I excited? Was World War II noisy? Upon hearing this news I immediately went to St. Mary's Catholic Church in Visalia. I was on my knees giving thanks. In retrospect, what I should have been praying for would later prove to be a real need for divine intervention.

Before accepting the new position, I telephoned the individual responsible for consummating the deal, a well-respected Los Angeles lawyer. I asked if there was anything about the new position or about the organization that I was contemplating joining that I needed to know. I mentioned I had purchased a new house with a basketball court (well, it was a slab of concrete outside my kitchen with a spotlight on the roof that was the Boston Gardens as far as I was concerned). I informed him that I had recently purchased a new car and that I was a single guy and I was enjoying the Southern California lifestyle. There was no reason for me to make a career change other than to pursue a more attractive opportunity. His reply was an emphatic endorsement of this position and the organization. There was nothing to be concerned about the lawyer went on; no surprises. Alas, I accepted the position.

Two weeks into my new position and I had not yet met the head of the union who was a major player in contract negotiations that funded the P.I.P.E. program. He was a powerful individual with a huge cache of industry clout. The one person who did not get involved in the interview process? That's him. We'll call this fellow Herb. I figured it was time to make Herb's

CHAPTER 1 – "You Won't Be Here Six Months!"

acquaintance and to tell him how excited I was to be a part of this industry. My appointment was set.

Herb's office was a short distance from mine. As I approached his office I thought about how I would tell him how enthused I was with my new position and explain some of the action steps I thought would lead the organization to new heights. I was pumped. I walked into his office and found him seated at his desk. He didn't greet me; he didn't say a word; he just kept on doing whatever he had been doing before I entered his office. I introduced myself. He still hadn't said anything. I proceeded to explain how glad I was to be in my new position and how I thought we could work together to make the programming all the better. His only reaction was no reaction.

As I was reciting my short monologue I noticed that he still wasn't looking at me. Herb just sat there in a strange type of stupor. I figured he must be waiting for my next eloquent remark before he welcomes me to the fold and tells me how pleased he is that I am a part of the Industry. As I was about to end my comments, he finally looked up and bellowed out: "You won't be here six months!" I looked around. I was certain someone had entered the room. It couldn't be me he was yelling at. I was sure there was someone behind me. There wasn't.

I left Herb's office with a new mandate: I needed a "Plan B". My "Plan A" was to do what I was hired to do. I could see this fellow was very interested in seeing my "Plan A" go up in flames. If I was going to successfully deal with this guy, I had to be on an equal playing field. I had an immediate need to have some form of security in order to deal with Herb. He had the leverage. He was a powerful fellow who was quite adept at intimidating those who got in his way.

My next move was to phone the Chairman of the Board of P.I.P.E. and explain that we had a problem personality to deal with. I reminded the Chairman how I had left a very secure management position with SCE and now found myself in a firestorm with a most difficult person. To get on an equal playing field with Herb, I needed some form of job security. I needed an employment contract, which I did not have. An employment contract, I felt, would nullify some of Herb's intimidating antics. California, like most states, is a right–to–work state, which basically means that an employer can terminate an employee at will. And that is exactly what Herb would love to be able to do to me. I got my contract. Round one went to Sabol. However, a 15-round, three-year fight was about to unfold.

A lesson I learned from my two short weeks into this experience, which would influence me throughout my career, is to have a "Plan B". You can do your pre-employment due diligence, which I did with the lawyer. You can have the best of intentions when making a career move, which I did. The upfront people – those whom you meet when interviewing and discussing employment opportunities – can be gracious and honorable people as were the P.I.P. E. Board of Trustees. You can do all of that and still run into problems. Everyone's "Plan B" may not include an employment contract. In fact many employers won't provide them. Astute professionals, however, can learn from the line delivered in the movie *Clear and Present Danger* by the fine actor James Earl Jones when he advises his new CIA replacement (played by Harrison Ford): *"Watch your back, Jack!"* Your "Plan B" needs to include the protection of your backside.

Herb devoted nearly every waking hour during the next three years trying his best to blaspheme, interrupt, destroy, complain, and chastise every initiative my staff and I attempted to introduce. The organization could have hired Mother Teresa for this job and Herb would have found fault with her. P.I.P.E. had been functioning for nearly two decades, but that didn't make any difference to Herb. His primary goal was to eliminate P.I.P.E. After three years he was successful in seeing that P.I.P.E. funding was dead meat. He had succeeded in eliminating P.I.P.E., but not before our programming had achieved substantial success.

Early in my position, I retained the research firm, Lieberman Research West in Century City, California to conduct benchmark research of market opinion regarding the image and the value of the union plumbing industry in Southern California. I wanted hard data to measure the effectiveness of the programming I was planning.

We created marketing, advertising, PR, and publicity programming designed to educate the Southern California market about the value of union mechanical contractors and union plumbers and pipe fitters. We created reoccurring segments on national TV – *The Dinah Shore Show* on CBS – where an Industry member demonstrated to Dina how to resolve a variety of household plumbing problems. Herb complained about that. We produced publicity highly favorable to the Industry in publications ranging from *The Los Angeles Times* to trade journals. He mocked that effort. We produced collateral material including a trade show booth, first-aid kits, bumper stickers, pencils, flags, hardhats, and more. Herb didn't like any of it. Our radio advertising was creative and stimulating. Good ol' Herb bitched about that. He even threatened to sue us. By now Herb was a full-fledged difficult and challenging person in my life.

Follow-up research by Lieberman documented significant increases in market awareness. We had achieved the promotional success we had sought. Our work was honored by the University of Southern California School of Business and the Sales and Marketing Executives Association of Southern California. Herb may have had the power to eliminate an organization, but my staff and I had the last laugh. Unfortunately, I don't know of any banks that credit your account for humor. So there I was, pleased with the success we had achieved, but I was sans employment. I began thinking, maybe those road trips up Interstate 99 to Visalia weren't so boring after all.

> "See those who cause us distress as valued teachers who provide us with opportunities to grow."
>
> Eastern Proverb

There was good news from my experience with P.I.P.E. The good news was that I was out on the street seeking new employment. Now some may find that a bit ironic. However, that experience with the union boss stimulated me to think in earnest about the value of communicating and dealing effectively with a difficult and challenging person. I wondered how many other people had a similar experience with a pain-in-the-rear like Herb. I certainly wasn't the only one on the planet to suffer through these experiences. And I was convinced that he would not be the last challenging individual I would have to deal with in my career.

If I wanted to deal effectively with these types of personalities in the future, I needed to do some searching. I began to think about what I could have done that I did not do that may have produced a more favorable outcome with this type of person. I set out from that moment on to acquire a body of knowledge that could be used to communicate with and to cope with a variety of personalities that I was certain would cross my path and the paths of others in the years to come. We all run into these personalities. Now it's time to learn how to effectively communicate and to deal with them. That's what this book is all about.

Chapter 2 – Conflict in the Workplace

> *"What we've got here is ...failure to communicate."*
> Captain, Road Prison 36
> *Cool Hand Luke* (1967)

Job stress is as much a business issue as it is a health issue. It costs American businesses hundreds of billions of dollars a year in employee burnout, turnover, higher absenteeism, lower production, and increased health-care costs. The American Psychological Association estimates that 60 percent of all absences are due to stress-related issues, costing U.S. companies more than *$57 billion a year.*

Perhaps the most costly and complicated job-stress related issue is employee conflict. Having to deal with difficult people creates stress. And eventually, the distraction of dealing with difficult people leads to lowered productivity among employers and employees alike. What a waste of precious resources!

High Costs of Workplace Conflict

Dr. David B. Lipsky, Director of the Institute on Conflict Resolution at Cornell University and President of the Labor and Employment Relations Association, identifies four types of costs associated with workplace conflict:

- **Direct dollar costs.** Simply put, co-worker conflict impacts an organization's bottom line. Productivity of goods and services interrupted or lost cuts into an employer's revenue. And if an employee bills for his services by the hour, such as lawyers, accountants, and other service firm professionals do, then the direct cost is the loss of a person's time – what the person should be earning but is not being paid because he or she is dealing with conflict.

- **Opportunities lost.** Co-worker conflict can have a major effect on an organization's potential to produce and achieve. Time devoted to resolving conflict takes away from an employee's better use of his or her time, talent, and effort. Consider what those involved in the conflict would otherwise be producing if they weren't wrapped up in the conflict. This is the opportunity lost.

- **Indirect costs.** Conflicts often involve innocent bystanders. Individuals do not have to be personally involved in workplace conflict to be impacted by it. Having to work in an environment where conflict exists often increases the stress levels of surrounding workers.

- **Personal and institutional relationships.** Emotions can run high during and after conflicts. Lingering anger or fear can drain productivity. Stressed co-workers often find their attitudes and their workplace behavior is affected even long after an event has occurred.

"Whenever the parties in a relationship do not share common values, objectives, and interests, conflict is likely to occur," Lipsky states. "In other words, conflict is inevitable in most relationships. That is not necessarily bad because constructive conflict can lead to innovative and durable solutions to problems that might not have been contemplated had the parties in the relationship shared the same values and objectives. Conflict cannot always be channeled in a positive direction, however, and its costs often outweigh its benefits."

Workplace Stress and The Rising Cost of Health Insurance

One of the single biggest expenses facing American business is the rising cost of health insurance. The Kaiser Family Foundation's 2006 Annual Employer Health Benefits Survey included 3,159 randomly selected public and private firms with three or more employees. While the survey reported a moderation in the rate of premium growth, the growth in health insurance costs outpaced the rate of inflation as well as workers' wages.

Reducing employee job stress could have a substantial positive impact on an organization's bottom line.

Unmanaged employee conflict is perhaps the largest reducible cost in organizations today – and probably the least recognized according to Daniel Dana, Ph.D., author and founder of Mediation Training Institute International based in Mission, Kansas. Dana reports that an estimated 65 percent of performance problems result from strained relationships between employees – not from deficiencies in an employee's skill or motivation.

Eight Conflict Cost Factors

To better understand how conflict at work impacts an organization's bottom line, Dana identifies eight cost factors:

1) **Wasted time**: Conflict distracts employees from otherwise productive use of their time. A study of managers in *Leadership Quarterly* showed that 42 percent of their time was spent reaching agreements with others instead of focusing on their work.

2) **Reduced decision quality**: Common sense would tell you that decisions made under conditions of conflict are most often inferior to decisions made when cooperation prevails. Good decisions must be based on optimum quantity and quality of

needed information. If information is withheld (as is examined in Chapter 11) or distorted by those who are depended upon to provide it, then the decision cannot be the best decision possible. If conflict is present between people who share decision-making authority, as in the case of team-based decisions, resulting decisions are likely to be contaminated by power contests.

3) **Loss of skilled employees:** Organizations invest in employees with compensation and training. Exit interviews reveal that chronic unresolved conflict is a decisive factor, Dana reports, in at least 50 percent of all voluntary employee departures.

4) **Restructuring:** When employees are in conflict, workflow is often altered in an attempt to reduce personal interaction between the employees in conflict. The restructured work is usually less efficient than the original design, which would have been satisfactory if the conflicting employees had been able to work together in the first place.

5) **Sabotage/theft/damage:** Studies reveal a direct correlation between employee conflict and the amount of damage or theft of inventory and equipment. When employees are angry with their employer, they are less inclined to care about a company's assets.
.

6) **Lowered job motivation:** Many employees experience erosion of job motivation due to stress associated with trying to get along with a perceived "difficult person."

7) **Lost work time:** There is a correlation between absenteeism and stress on the job, especially when stress is associated with anger toward coworkers. This stress, combined with disregard for how one's absence impacts others, can lead to employees choosing to take time off – sometimes excused as a "sick day."

8) **Health costs:** Illness and injuries requiring medical attention are partially psychogenic, i.e., mentally or emotionally induced, and conflict contributes to their psychogenesis. Since the rate of claims affects the premium paid by an employer to its insurer, insurance is an indirect cost of workplace conflict.

To calculate the financial costs that a particular conflict creates, Dana provides an excellent "Cost Estimation Worksheet" in his revealing book, *Managing Differences.*

The Impact of Stress on Productivity

Anyone who works for a living – and that includes most of us – experiences some form of workplace stress. After all, it's work, not a midday siesta. However, high levels of stress are not good –

for employees or employers. According to a survey conducted by ComPsych, a U.S.-based provider of employee assistance programs, more than half of all workers are experiencing high levels of stress at work – and it's having a substantial impact on attendance as well as productivity. The survey revealed that 55 percent of workers have high levels of stress, "with extreme fatigue/feeling out of control."

While these figures are troubling, consider the following findings regarding the impact of stress on productivity:

- 40 percent of respondents said they lose one hour or more *per day* in productivity due to stress

- 48 percent come to work one to four days per year too stressed to be effective, and an additional 25 percent come to work too stressed to be effective five or more days per year

- 47 percent miss work one or two days per year due to stress and an additional 33 percent miss three to six days per year.

At the center of this stress is the behavior of people and their ability or inability to communicate. Some 36 percent of respondents said that "people issues" were the primary cause of their stress. This figure was up eight percent from the survey conducted in the first half of 2006.

According to the *Denver Business Journal*, most managers spend at least 15 percent of their time dealing with "personality" squabbles that good interpersonal communication skills and supporting communications could help mediate.

Worth noting is research on the lack of respect in the workplace conducted by Christine L. Porath, Ph.D., assistant professor in the Management and Organization department at the USC Marshall School of Business, and Christine M. Pearson, associate professor of management at Thunderbird – The Garvin School of International Management. They point out that "incivility," or employees' lack of regard for one another, is costly to organizations in subtle and pervasive ways.

"Over the past eight years, as we have learned about this phenomenon through interviews, focus groups, questionnaires, experiments, and executive forums with more than 2,400 people across the U.S. and Canada, we have found that incivility causes its targets, witnesses, and additional stakeholders to act in ways that erode organizational values and deplete organizational resources," Porath and Pearson state.

The impact of rude behavior affects more than morale and employee attitude. It hits the bottom line. "Among survey respondents, one target in eight left the job to escape a troublesome uncivil situation," according to Porath and Pearson.

"With fully loaded costs of turnover estimated at 1.5 to 2.5 times the salary paid for the job, or $50,000 per existing employee across all jobs and industries in the U.S., the bottom-line effects of incivility are far from trivial."

Job Turnover

Similar findings are supported by other notable sources. Costs of employee turnover, according to *mediate.com* authors Cynthia Barnes-Slater and John Ford, can be grouped into five major categories:

1. Severance costs – voluntary or involuntary
2. Benefits costs – compensation, etc.
3. Recruitment and staffing cycle time costs
4. Training and development costs
5. Lost productivity costs.

"In addition to these costs resulting from employee turnover is the psychological cost to employees," Ford says. "When employees leave because of rude behavior among employees or from job stress, other employees can be adversely affected. Their morale can be lowered when they see coworkers leave."

Besides losing quality people due to workplace stress caused by problem employees, another issue presents itself in the form of "presenteeism." This occurs when employees have strong intentions of leaving an organization but fail to do so. These folks just sort of hang around on the job at a substantial cost to their employer.

"Such employees tend to have lower commitment, be more dissatisfied with their jobs, and reduce morale in the area in which they work," according to the *Duxbury & Higgins, Work-Life Conflict in Canada in the New Millenium: A Status Report, 2003.*

These people end up "retiring on the job," which contributes to workload problems for others in their area.

"The rate of 'presenteeism' is estimated to be as much as three times higher than absenteeism," according to *WarrenShepel [online] Health & Wellness Research Database, 2005.*

"There is no escaping the reality that job performance is impacted by the relationships that people have at work," explains Ron Goetzel, director of the Cornell Institute for Health and Productivity Studies (IHPS). "Poor relationships can result from conflict between coworkers, which contributes to presenteeism. When people are under stress caused by friction with coworkers, they are less likely to devote 100% of their attention and effort to the job at hand."

Stress in the Balance

Experts readily acknowledge the negative impact that conflict and stress can create at work. However, not all conflict and stress is bad.

"Increased stress increases productivity – up to a point. After which things rapidly deteriorate, and that level also differs for each of us," explains Paul J. Rosch, M.D., F.A.C.P., and President of the American Institute of Stress.

"It's much like the stress or tension on a violin string. Not enough produces a dull raspy sound; too much, an irritating screech or snaps the string. But just the correct degree of stress creates a beautiful tone. Similarly, we all have to find the right amount of stress that permits us to make pleasant music in our daily lives. You can learn to use and transform stress, so it will make you more productive and less self-destructive."

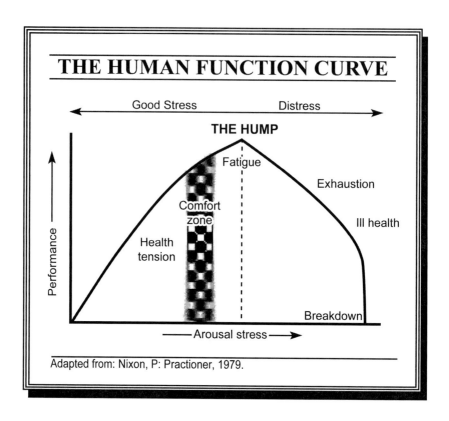

Source: *The American Institute of Stress (AIS)*

As illustrated above, increased stress results in increased productivity – up to a point. After which things rapidly go downhill. However, that point or peak differs for each of us, so you need to be sensitive to the early warning symptoms that suggest a stress overload. Such signals also differ for each of us and can be so subtle that we often ignore them until it's too late.

Infrequently, others are aware that you may be headed for trouble before you are.

Numerous studies show that job stress is by far the major source of stress for American adults. And according to *The American Institute of Stress,* stress has escalated progressively over the past few decades. Increased levels of job stress, as assessed by the perception of having little control but lots of demands, have been demonstrated to be associated with increased rates of heart attack, hypertension, and other disorders.

You can learn more about your own job stress level by answering the following ten questions:

How Much Job Stress Do You Have?

ENTER NUMBERS FROM THE SLIDING SCALE THAT BEST DESCRIBE YOU
STRONGLY DISAGREE   AGREE SOMEWHAT   STRONGLY AGREE   1   2   3   4   5   6   7   8   9   10
I can't honestly say what I really think or get things off my chest at work.   ____
My job has a lot of responsibility, but I don't have very much authority   ____
I could usually do a much better job if I were given more time   ____
I seldom receive adequate acknowledgment or appreciation when my work is really good.   ____
In general, I am not particularly proud or satisfied with my job.   ____
I have the impression that I am repeatedly picked on or discriminated against at work.   ____
My workplace environment is not very pleasant or particularly safe.   ____
My job often interferes with my family and social obligations or personal needs.   ____
I tend to have frequent arguments with superiors, coworkers, or customers.   ____
Most of the time, I feel that I have very little control over my life at work.   ____
Add up the replies to each question for your TOTAL STRESS SCORE.

If you score between 10 and 30, you handle stress on your job well; between 40 and 60, moderately well; 70 and 100, you're encountering problems that need to be addressed and resolved.

If you experience too much stress – when the flood of hormones bombards your body longer than 24 hours – all kinds of bad things start to happen. According to a November 2006 *MSNBC.com* report, long-term, chronic emotional stress can lead to high blood pressure, heart disease, exhaustion, and depression.

"Over time, if you're constantly in fight-or-flight, if your heart muscles and valves are awash in the epinephrine, it causes changes in the arteries and in the way cells are able to regenerate," says Dr. Lynne Tan, Medical Director at Montefiore Medical Center in White Plains, New York. "Constant conflict (stress) within an organization (macrocosm) works in a similar way to constant stress within an organism (microcosm). It breaks down the immune system of the body due to the stress hormones that are secreted and the changes that occur in the HPA (hypothalamic-pituitary adrenal) axis over the long term. Likewise, the strength of an organization is dependent on the strength and productivity of its many parts (i.e., workers).

"If people are working in stressful environments caused by ineffective problem-solving and conflict resolution on the part of management, they may manifest physical, emotional, and mental illnesses due to constant stress," according to Tan. "The human body is not made to live in constant stress. Any stress that lingers beyond 24-48 hours causes the body to undergo negative changes."

Organizations and the people they employ are at risk from the slings and arrows of their daily lives. Reducing unneeded stress and eliminating related costs are achieved when we know how to communicate effectively and to deal appropriately with difficult and challenging personalities.

Fortunately, this book will provide you with the tools you'll need in these difficult types of situations. In Chapter Five, for example, you'll learn how to create effective communications with difficult people. And in Chapter Seven, we'll examine eight activities to improve our relationships with such individuals.

Chapter 3 – Understanding The Difficult Personality

> "Gentlemen... You can't fight in here! This is the War Room!"
> Dr. Strangelove (1964)

Business retreats are held regularly throughout the world with agendas designed to educate and inspire employees to excel in their daily routines. But how many agendas include a segment to educate individuals on how to communicate and deal with difficult people? Those who can afford it, and perhaps a few who cannot, pay to have a personal trainer make certain they get out of bed in the morning to work out and stay physically fit. But how many of those individuals think of investing a little time and energy to learn how to deal with people who cause stress at work and in their personal lives?

Understanding difficult personalities may not reduce your waist size, nor trim your thighs, but it can make work more pleasant and home life more enjoyable. Understanding the difficult person positions us to determine the best course of action to take to become proficient in our communications with challenging personalities. Therefore, we need to get inside the other person's head before we choose a course of action because prescription without proper diagnosis gives way to communications malpractice.

One of the first steps towards understanding difficult personalities is to get a sense as to why they are the way they are. Why are some bosses just plain difficult to be around when other bosses are a delight? According to Roy H. Lubit, M.D., Ph.D. and author of *Coping With Toxic Managers*, the better you understand how other people view their world and what motivates them, the better you will be able to influence them to behave in ways that are helpful. Your goal is not to play psychiatrist hoping to create massive personality changes in the difficult person. Your goal is to be aware that there are root causes for the person's communications and behavior style, and to consider these causes when responding to the challenges these personalities present.

Personality traits can contribute to exceptional communications and difficult behavior. Attention Deficit Hyperactivity Disorder (ADHD) can contribute to aggressive behavior, including yelling. Family background can be a root cause of caustic communications. An individual raised in a family of aggressive language and/or behavior will often bring that demeanor to the work environment.

An organization's culture will likely have an impact on the number of challenging personnel it employs. Those who lead organizations serve as role models of behavior and communications. Unfortunately, the model they set is often grounded in their work experience and is void of any formal education in dealing with difficult people. This is particularly true within professional service firms where leaders are chosen for reasons that do not always support their ability to manage people and to resolve communications conflicts. Those who serve in law, accounting, architect and engineering firms, among other professional services, are highly technically skilled professionals. They may or may not have had any formal education in communication and people management. Many of those in management serve as a role model in reverse – you learn from them by observing their shortcomings and by learning what **not** to do when dealing with difficult and challenging personalities.

The Dollar Bill Story

A highly regarded intellectual property lawyer joined the New York office as a lateral partner of a large prestigious international law firm. In addition to bringing to the firm a reputation as a leading IP lawyer, he also brought baggage – a well-earned reputation for being a difficult and challenging personality. When the firm's executive director, a former McKinsey and Company partner, Stanford MBA, and a respected executive, was scheduling his agenda for meetings in the New

York office, the newly joined IP partner asked the executive director to bring to their meeting 100 one-dollar bills.

As the two met for the first time, the partner asked if the executive director had brought the 100 one-dollar bills as he had requested. The executive director replied that he had, and was then instructed to begin placing one of the dollar bills on the partner's desk. As they began their meeting in the partner's office, he would intermittently instruct the executive director to place another dollar bill on the desk. This continued for a few minutes. The partner then abruptly stated: "A dollar every eight seconds is my billing rate. You're wasting my time. Now there's the door!" The point is this: The most well-intended organizations can still find their way to attracting very difficult people.

There are a variety of root causes of difficult behavior. Keep in mind when communicating and when coping with challenging personalities that their behavior is seldom ever personal. Your challenge is to be smart and flexible enough to deal effectively with the most difficult and challenging bosses, subordinates or colleagues.

Your Attitude Is Important

Your attitude dictates how smart and how flexible you will be when faced with the challenging personality. When you are faced

CHAPTER 3 – Understanding The Difficult Personality

with a difficult person you have choices: You can accept this behavior, hoping it will go away never to return or you can confront it. Some people avoid the stress of attempting to create change in the difficult person's behavior. Creating change for the better is not always easy. Some prefer to just tolerate difficult behavior.

When I asked the administrative manager of a professional service firm client in the U.S. if she had received regular performance appraisals, she replied that she had not, and added that the only time she heard from her superiors was when they yelled at her. She had been with her employer for 17 years and certain members were still yelling at her.

You are responsible for what you do and do not allow. No one controls you unless you allow it. Want 17 more years of being yelled at? If not, change your attitude and take the action required to remedy the situation. Beginning with Chapter 8 we will learn how to improve relationships with bosses, co-workers, and other challenging personalities.

Chapter 4 – Are You Sure It's The Other Guy?

> *"It's a little like looking into a mirror and trying to see what you look like when you're not really looking at your own reflection."*
> Ross McElwee
> *Sherman's March* (1986)

Before pointing fingers and seeking a solution to any perceived communication or coping challenges, we must begin with a thorough self-examination. We need to take a serious look in the mirror. Are you certain that the source for the communications challenges or behavioral problems you experience is the other person, and not you? What exactly is your mirror telling you?

Have you experienced problems with people in the past? If so, have the problems stemmed from one particular type of person? Was there an issue for you with the person's age, gender, religion, political beliefs? Have you had encounters at work requiring intervention from senior management? If your answer is *yes* to any of these questions, your mirror is telling you of a need to solve your personal issues before seeking a resolution with the other person.

Are you sure that the other person is really the problem and that you're not overreacting? Does a pattern exist for you in your interaction with co-workers? Do you recognize that you have hot buttons that are easily pushed? – we all have them. If so, you need to be honest with yourself and make adjustments in your behavior that will foster favorable relations.

Most people who get fired for non-economic reasons don't get the boot for doing a bad job, but because they lack the human relationship skills to work with others.

Even if a person's troublemaking doesn't get him fired, it could ruin his chances for promotions or sizeable pay increases. If he is someone people can't stand, chances are he is not going to go far in most organizations.

One person's co-worker from hell could be an ideal match for another employee. If you are the type of person who needs regular direction and is slow in making decisions, you will be miserable with a controlling type of person. However, if you have a strong need for autonomy you will likely flourish with this type of person. Before you conclude that a fellow employee is a big problem, think again. The behavior that you see as irritating may be nothing more than a chemistry issue. The other person may be very effective and blends well with everyone else.

One of our first steps is to determine if the object of our attention is the other person's attitude or his actions. Some people possess a positive attitude that seems to lift others around them. They always have a bright outlook on life and work. These people are enjoyable to be with because they get along well with others. And then there are the *downers* - those folks who just seem to bring down everyone around them. Nothing seems to satisfy them. They're skilled at finding fault where fault does not exist. Don't let that person's attitude get to you. Spending your time and energy trying to change that person's attitude for the better is most likely a waste of your time and energy. Limit your time with these types of people.

Those who are effective in communicating with difficult people make it their goal to listen and understand first before attempting to be heard and understood. Do you create an environment conducive for effective communications by focusing your attention and your energy on the other person? When you assist the other person to express himself completely, you increase the potential for him to hear you. When the other person is convinced that you are seriously hearing and responding objectively to what he is saying, he is inclined to lower those barriers that are impeding communications between the two of you. Are you truly listening to what the other person has to say? Needless to say you don't have to agree with any of his messages; but you do have a responsibility to help create an environment of open and unencumbered communications. What reflection are you getting now from your mirror?

Performance reviews can be a great help in acquiring a better understanding of one's own behavior and attitude. What do your performance reviews say about your attitude, your behavior, and your personal communications skills? You don't need an exhausting 360 degree review of yourself, but you do need to obtain objective feedback to determine if you may be the source of any problems with the other person. What reflection are you receiving from your performance reviews?

There are a variety of resources available to assist one to acquire a better understanding of one's own behavior. Counseling associations worth noting include the following:

American Counseling Association – Offers a series of articles directed to the general public, and the articles are designed to help educate individuals about potential problems, when it might be appropriate to seek counseling assistance, and the role a counselor might play. (http://www.counseling.org).

APA Help Center – The American Psychological Association offers useful facts, information, and advice on how psychological services can help people cope with problems such as stress, depression, family strife, or chronic illness. The site provides sections devoted to psychology in the workplace, the health implications of the mind/body connection, family and personal relationships, and psychology in daily life. (http://helping.apa.org).

National Board of Certified Counselors – Offers services to help people find an appropriate counseling professional in their area. (http://www.nbcc.org).

National Career Development Association – Offers information for consumers on what to look for in a counselor, what to expect when you pursue counseling, and a list of approved Master Career Counselors (MCC) and Master Career Development Professionals (MCDP). (http://www.ncda.org).

In addition to associations that offer various services, you may want to consider taking a self-assessment test to help you learn more about yourself. Self-assessment testing helps determine what you like, what you don't like, and how you tend to react to certain situations. Knowing these things can help you determine which occupations and work situations could be a better fit for you.

There are many varieties of assessment tools, easily measuring a particular facet of your interests, skills, personality, and values. In addition to the associations listed above that can provide information on self-assessment tools, the following are additional self-assessment resources:

UCLA – (http://career.ucla.edu/explore/discover.asp)
University of Waterloo –
(http://www.cdm.uwaterloo.ca/step1asp?priNav=1)
UNC at Wilmington –
(http://www.uncwil.edu/stuaff/career/students/assessments.htm)
Science Next Wave – (http://sciencecareers.sciencemag.org)
Answering The Question Who Am I? –
(http://sciencecareers.sciencemag.org)
Career Zone – (http://www.nycareerzone.org)

Self-assessment tools require interpretive assistance or they are self-directed. *Interpretive Assistance* means that your results will have to be discussed with a person licensed or trained in this particular tool so you can understand what the data is saying. The cost of the tool will include this interpretive assistance in some form.

Self-Directed means the tool is designed so you can use it and review your results without a licensed or trained professional interpreting the data for you. Even though they do not *require* intervention to read the results, you may still find you have questions. If that is the case, the service offering the tool may offer a way for you to follow-up or you can turn to the associations above for help in finding a counselor.

> Just how flexible are you?

Some folks seem to resemble rubber bands in their relationships with co-workers. They are adept at adjusting to the most trying people and difficult circumstances. Others are not quite as flexible. The more flexible you are, the greater your likelihood of maintaining an amicable relationship with the difficult person. Knowing the level of your of flexibility and the level of flexibility of your co-worker provides you with valuable information for dealing with difficult and challenging co-workers. By completing the following ©*Flexibility – Self-Perception* assessment questionnaire (Exhibit 4), you will have identified your level of flexibility among 12 characteristics.

Place an "x" on each continuum as to where you believe you fall. Place a "y" on the continuum as to where you believe your co-worker falls. The number "1" represents a lower degree of flexibility and the number "4" represents a greater degree of flexibility. The greater the variance between your score on each of the 12 characteristics and those of the other person, the greater the likelihood of conflict you will experience with the other person. By adjusting your behavior in those characteristics that contain the greatest variance between yourself and your co-worker, you will increase the potential for a more harmonious relationship with the other person.

For further information on the application of the Flexibility-Self-Perception Questionnaire, contact Persona Global at *www.personaglobal.com.*

Exhibit 4

	1	2	3	4	
Uncooperative	___	___	___	___	Cooperative
Blunt	___	___	___	___	Appreciative
Manipulative	___	___	___	___	Genuine
Fixed	___	___	___	___	Adaptable
Rambling	___	___	___	___	Articulate
Stubborn	___	___	___	___	Agreeable
Undependable	___	___	___	___	Dependable
Awkward	___	___	___	___	Graceful
Lazy	___	___	___	___	Industrious
Self-oriented	___	___	___	___	Other-oriented
Sloppy	___	___	___	___	Orderly
Disrespectful	___	___	___	___	Respectful
Now total each column					
Totals	___	___	___	___	
	1	2	3	4	

Chapter 5 – Taking Personal Communications To The Next Level

> *"Hey Corporal, drop dead! And another thing, whenever you salute the Captain you make him an open target for the Germans so don't do it, especially when I'm standing near him!"*
>
> Private Adrian Caparzo
> *Saving Private Ryan* (1998)

If we want to improve our communications with those who make our days difficult, we need to understand how these three components impact our ability to create positive behavioral change:

- Words, images, and sounds
- Listening
- Communications styles

Words, images, and sounds

Understanding as much as we can about how and what the other person may be thinking enables us to communicate more effectively with the challenging personality. When preparing to communicate with the difficult person, ask yourself what you think his or her response to each of these questions would be.

These three questions can provide you with insight into the emotional composition of the other person: What do you *know* about what is taking place? What do you *think* about what is taking place? How do you *feel* about what is taking place?

One audience's reaction to the acclaimed film, *Saving Private Ryan*, speaks literally and loudly about our first component: *words, images,* and *sounds*. By themselves, words, images, and sounds mean very little in the communications process. They take on meaning as they are being interpreted by someone. A person's interpretation of those words, images, and sounds depends on age, education, and life experiences, among other criteria. The very same words or images or sounds can mean completely different things to different people.

Anyone who has seen *Saving Private Ryan* is aware of the graphic details leaping from the screen during the opening minutes of this film. Those responsible for this film went to great and successful lengths (the film won five academy awards) to capture the realism of the battle of the 2nd Ranger Battalion as it battled on June 6, 1944, at Omaha Beach in WWII. I viewed this film at the Odeon Theater in Leeds, England one Saturday evening and was stunned to hear laughter coming from various spots in the theater. I doubt that the producers of this film had any intention of generating humor in the opening scenes. I turned around to see what was happening. There was laughter coming from teenagers and youngsters, who found these gruesome scenes amusing. At the same time I noticed that older members of the audience – those with gray hair or perhaps no hair – sat transfixed in silence watching intently. The images and sounds heard by the kids were the same as those experienced by older folks. Yet the reactions generated by these bombastic images and sounds were extreme opposites. These opposites pinpoint how the differences in background experiences affect our communications.

The audience was split in its reactions to what they were experiencing. Why? Because of their backgrounds. Differences in backgrounds create one of the primary barriers to intended communications.

Intended communications are affected by the age, education, gender, economic status, religion, temperament, cultural background, health, political beliefs, and even one's vocabulary.

The life experiences that younger members of that audience would recall while viewing this film were limited to what they learned in school or may have read on their own, viewed on TV or were told to them by relatives. The older folks in that theater may have had personal experiences with WWII or had a close relative with personal experience. More than 70 Leeds residents were killed during night bombing in WWII. How many of the youngsters do you think know of this or thought of this as they reacted to what they were seeing on that movie screen?

If the younger and the older audience members in that theater had been asked what they *knew, thought,* and *felt* about what was taking place, I am convinced they would have produced completely different answers, even though everyone saw and heard the same images and sounds.

Differences in how we react to various forms of communications are not limited to what we see and hear at movies. Simple words can produce completely different reactions. The word "go," for example, can have a completely different meaning depending on how the word is delivered. With great emphasis you can demand that a person "Go!" because you want him out of your sight. You can pose the same two letters in the form of a question as in "Go?" meaning "I really don't want you to leave." The same word has two completely different interpretations.

When Herb exclaimed to me, "You won't be here six months!", I could have interpreted that to mean that I would be promoted in six months. Six months from now, great opportunities will come my way. How lucky can a guy get! However, that was not what he had in mind for me. Different words can mean different things to different people.

Listening

> "The most basic and powerful way to connect to another person is to listen. Perhaps the most important thing we ever give each other is our attention."
>
> Rachel Naomi Remen

There is a correlation between a vital listening experience of mine and the assassination of Martin Luther King. Let me explain. While going through basic training in the Army at Fort Polk, Louisiana, I was in charge of a platoon of forty-six trainee soldiers – about half of whom were African American and about half Caucasian. The day Dr. King was assassinated – April 4, 1968 – was also our last day of basic training. This meant that all of us were to be assigned that day to our next gig – or as the military preferred to call it: Military Occupational Specialty (MOS).

Many of the African American soldiers in my platoon enlisted for three years – as opposed to being drafted for two years – with the understanding that they would likely be given their MOS of choice. This was taking place during the height of the Viet Nam War. The next stop for those assigned to Infantry for their MOS was almost certain to be Viet Nam. Guess where nearly all of those who had signed up for the three years learned on that fateful day where they were being sent for their MOS? –

Tiger Land! No, Tiger Land was not a habitat at Disney's Animal Kingdom. Tiger Land was the Infantry Training Center at Fort Polk. Talk about the Bandini hitting the fan! Coupling the emotional impact of the assassination of Dr. King with not receiving the assignment they expected after enlisting for three years, turned our barracks that night into a near riot. One trainee was hit in the back with a pipe and relations between races were about to explode. What should have never been a racial issue was now a full-blown racial issue.

The solution, I believed at the time, was to figure a way to release some of the pressure that was boiling over. I called for a meeting with the leaders of the uprising and quickly found myself to be one of only two non-African Americans in a room with a dozen or so very unhappy African American soldiers. As I began the meeting, I wasn't sure if I would succeed in quelling emotions or if I would be making a quick exit to the infirmary for medical attention. So I listened. They yelled. I listened. They ranted. I listened some more. The more I kept quiet and focused on *how* they expressed their anger and pain, the more effective our communications became, and the more emotions subsided. We all left the next day for our MOS assignments. It didn't take a rocket scientist to understand *why* they were mad. What it did take was an opportunity for them to have someone listen to them.

Effective listening becomes important to us when we realize it is the first step in transforming the challenging personality into a collaborative colleague. Active, empathetic, and responsive listening takes place when we genuinely care about what the other person is trying to tell us and actively reach out with questions, tone, voice, and body language. When people feel that they have not been heard, it only adds to their frustration and anger adding fuel to the difficult person's combustible personality.

> *"When people talk, listen completely. Most people never listen."*
> Ernest Hemingway

While most of us realize the value of listening skills, few, in my experience, have done anything about it. I have asked some 2,000 professionals in seven countries – lawyers, accountants, airline executives, electric utility company personnel, dental hygienists, college students, and PR and marketing professionals – how many have taken a course, read a book, listened to an audio tape, or viewed a videotape on listening skills. The response was a deafening two percent. Many of those I have asked are college graduates, some with post-graduate degrees.

Authors Lyman K. Steil and Richard K. Bommelje, point out in their book, *Listening Leaders*, that listening and leadership are inseparable because listening is the best way to learn about the true needs, expectations, and desires of followers. "As leaders advance in their level of responsibility, the importance of listening increases dramatically. In short, listening is central to the personal and professional success of all leaders, at all levels, and in all endeavors," Steil and Bommelje state.

Steil and Bommelje further report that immediately after listening to a ten-minute presentation, the average listener hears, correctly understands, properly evaluates, stores, and appropriately responds to approximately half of what is said. They further point out that within forty-eight hours, the figure drops to a final effectiveness level of twenty-five percent.

Little wonder that communication breakdowns lead to conflict in the workplace. Common sense tells us that the same inefficient listening skills present at work are brought home waiting to be exorcised by one's spouse, child, or other household member.

Why We Don't Listen

We know that effective listening is important. So why don't we listen? Here are a few reasons:

•*We are not trained to listen.* Listening is not a part of our educational system. A private high school in Orlando, Florida offers a Marine Biology course that provides students with an

CHAPTER 5 - Taking Personal Communications To The Next Level   49

opportunity to swim right next to manatees, which is the only reason my daughter took the course. What about a course on listening? Not to be found.

• *The mind is elsewhere.* While we speak at the rate of 125 to 150 words per minute, we can comprehend approximately 500 words per minute. This variance creates a comprehension thought gap. The body is present. The mind is elsewhere.

Since we are capable of receiving so much more information than the sender is giving us, we can simultaneously think about a variety of subjects that have nothing to do with what the other person intends for us to receive. When we listen, the spoken words arrive at slow speed, our brain works with hundreds of additional words assembling many thoughts other than those spoken to us. We can think about our work schedule. We can think about how our favorite sports team is doing. There are countless ways in which one's attention can be focused on anything other than what the other person has to say.

> *No communication – written or oral – guarantees the attention of the recipient.*

While participating in a seminar held at the Biltmore Hotel in Los Angeles a while back, I watched the majority of an audience of several hundred strain to remain awake as one presentation tried to out-bore the other. During the first break of the day, with the audience downing one cup of coffee after another to fend off any narcoleptic tendencies, curiosity got the best of me. I had the distinct feeling that a goodly number of the audience was not paying attention to the presentations. What I found as I walked through the aisles did not surprise me. Rather than finding copious notes of the morning's proceedings, I observed some of the best doodling I had ever seen. Want a nice drawing of a dog or cat? How about some nice X's and O's? They were all there. The audience members were present. Their minds were elsewhere.

A study conducted by MCI found that more than 11 million meetings occur in U.S. business every day. The study [*Meetings in America: A study of trends, costs, and attitudes toward business travel, teleconferencing, and their impact on productivity*] indicated that employees attended an average of 61.8 meetings each month and that 91 percent of those attending these meetings acknowledged that they daydreamed and that 39 percent said they dozed off during meetings. Do you think any of those who were daydreaming or who dozed off were listening well?

• *I am in control when I am talking.* If you happen to be an expert in the subject of discussion, you know that there is a natural tendency for many people to take the lead and to talk about that which they know well. If we are good at what we do, we like to talk about it. If we think we know more about the subject of discussion, we like to talk about it. If we have a strong opinion on a subject – especially if the subject strikes an emotional cord with us – we talk. It's quite difficult to listen when we talk.

• *I am thinking ahead.* By anticipating what we will say next, we risk not receiving the message the other person intended. We may be so intent on responding to the other person that our focus is not on what he is saying. Our focus is on the message we are mentally crafting. When we fail to receive the other person's message, we send our own message back that what he has to say is not important.

• *I'm comfortable when I talk.* Hey, if people will listen, others will talk, particularly about themselves and their careers. Look at people on their cell phones. What are they doing? They're talking. Does anyone listen anymore? Wendell Johnson, author of *Your Most Enchanted Listener*, points out: "People seem to be far more powerfully driven to talk at each other than to listen to each other, and when they do listen, the kind of feedback they give the speaker – and the kind of reaction the speaker makes, in turn, to this feedback – appears distressingly often to be self-defensive and generally competitive or insincere and thus misleading, rather than clarifying, honest, and co-operative."

Make Listening Your Ally

Our personal experiences, culture, education, economic background, and family composition, among other factors, impact our interpretation of information as it is given to us. We filter and interpret this information based on our experiences, needs, interests, and expectations. Effective listening acknowledges these filters and helps us to shape the messages we deliver in return. The more effective we are in listening to these clues, the more effective we are in speaking the language of the other person. Listening, then, remains key to two-way communications.

> *Effective listening makes you a better presenter of your ideas and thoughts and your overall message.*

Here are a few tips on how to make your listening a great communications resource:

1. *Prepare to listen:* The first step in communicating – especially with challenging personalities – is not listening. The important first step to effective listening is _preparing_ to listen, which means

to become physically alert and to think of the value you will receive from the information that is about to be presented. Whether you may agree with or disagree with what you hear, the point is this: There is something of value for you to listen to in the information to be presented. Otherwise, why are you there?

2. *Think "white board":* Empty yourself of any preconceived ideas. Drop predefined roles, and let go of agendas, assumptions, judgments, and expectations – of everything that might twist what you will hear into something other than what was intended. Think of your mind as a "white board" with no markings of any kind. Wipe away any feelings, emotions, or attitudes. With a pristine white board you are now ready to receive the information accurately and post it to your new white board.

3. *Zero in with your mind:* Pay close attention. Think along with the speaker by listening to the main ideas. Don't get bogged down with the details. Ralph G. Nicholls, recognized as the "father of the field of listening" and co-author along with Leonard A Stephens of the classic book *Are You Listening?*, points out that many people take pride in being able to say that above all they try to "get the facts" when they listen. "When people talk, they want listeners to understand their *ideas*. The facts are useful chiefly for constructing the ideas. Grasping ideas,

we have found, is the skill on which the good listener concentrates. He remembers facts only long enough to understand the ideas that are built from them," the authors state. "But then, almost miraculously, grasping an idea will help the listener to remember the supporting facts more effectively than does the person who goes after facts alone." This listening skill is one which definitely can be taught, one in which people can build experience leading toward improved aural communications.

4. *Demonstrate your understanding:* Respond to the other person with more than just saying, "I understand." People need some sort of evidence or proof of your understanding. Provide meaningful feedback to the other person by occasionally restating the main points or by asking a question that proves you understand the main idea. If you don't understand the other person's idea, that's all the more reason to ask questions. The important point is not to repeat what they've said to prove you were listening, but to prove you understand. The difference in these two intentions transmits remarkably different messages when you are communicating.

5. *Eliminate emotions:* Our listening abilities are impacted by our emotions. If we hear something that opposes our most deeply held ideas, concepts, or convictions, we send up a barrier as we

prepare a response to what we are hearing. We turn off our reception, at the risk of missing vital information. Emotion also comes into play when we hear something we especially like and with which we agree. When this occurs our listening fails us as we risk accepting everything we hear including truths, half-truths, and fiction. Our listening becomes distorted as we seek to reinforce our preconceived beliefs and concepts. The solution to both forms of emotion, which requires self-control, is to withhold evaluation of the information presented. Hold off making judgments. After the person has finished presenting his or her thoughts, review the main ideas presented, and then assess them.

6. *Search for the negative:* A natural tendency is to listen for information that supports our ideas and beliefs. After all, we like to be around people whose views agree with our own. Seldom do we seek out information that opposes our beliefs. A method for improving our listening skills is to search for the negative – that information that hits us where it may hurt. As Ralph Nicholls states in his book *Are You Listening?*: "If we make up our minds to seek out the ideas that might prove us wrong, as well as those that might prove us right, we are less in danger of missing what people have to say."

7. *Take notes:* I distinctly recall asking two partners at a prestigious law firm in the United Kingdom if they took notes when they met with clients or with prospects. One lawyer responded that he always takes notes because he doesn't have a perfect memory and he doesn't want to risk missing important information. Contrasting that response was the other lawyer who said he does not take notes because he does not want others to think that he doesn't have a great memory. Their response reminds me of the old adage: "We all have photographic memories; it's just that some of us don't have any film."

How many times have you gone to a meeting thinking that you will remember the important things, only to find yourself asking a colleague for information about issues discussed during that session? Here is my recommendation: Unless you have a photographic memory with a lot of film, put your ego aside and take notes.

"We have discovered leaders' effectiveness increases dramatically with training and advancement in listening and taking more effective notes," authors Steil and Bommelje point out. "Finally, there is one observable, measurable and definite difference in the way listening leaders and poor listeners takes notes. The single major difference is, effective listeners take notes; ineffective listeners do not." Take notes!

If one is committed to creating effective communications with the difficult and challenging person, then understanding communications style is a priceless asset. Understanding an individual's personality and communications style allows a person to more effectively communicate and to persuade others to his or her point of view. Let's turn our attention to learning how communications styles can help a person communicate and relate more effectively.

Communications styles

Our communications with anyone – and particularly with the challenging personality – can be substantially improved by understanding the importance of personal communications styles. Studies have shown that people respond differently depending on the way in which the communications is conducted. People with different personalities communicate differently.

Your responsibility in the persuasion process is to learn to recognize each communications style and adjust how you present your message so that it will be acceptable to the person you want to persuade. Understanding an individual's communications style allows us to achieve the following:

- Build the rapport and trust required for successful communications

- Identify how the challenging person with whom you communicate likes to communicate

- Identify the kind of information people you want to convince, take notice of, and remember

- Identify how the people you want to influence make decisions

- Speak the language of your audience

All of these are important, but speaking the language of your audience has special meaning. Knowing how to relate, whether to one person or to an audience of thousands, has separated the well intended from the successful.

In the early 1970s, the People's Lobby, an environmental activist group, was successful in qualifying Proposition 9 – The Clean Environment Act – on the California election ballot. The goal of Proposition 9 was to end nuclear power as a source of energy in the United States. California was the test state.

This was an era when emotions were running high among a growing populous to end nuclear power as a source of electric energy in California. The stakes were high in the outcome of this pending election. Thousands of jobs were vulnerable and businesses of all sizes would be affected. In addition, electric service to millions of residences could be at risk.

Southern California Edison, my employer at the time, was a leader in structuring a communications effort to counter

CHAPTER 5 - Taking Personal Communications To The Next Level

Proposition 9, which included having select Edison employees speak to audiences throughout Southern California. Those chosen to be out in front speaking were highly educated engineers and technical experts, many with graduate and post-graduate degrees. They could describe the inner workings of a pressurized water reactor and the physical makeup of spent fuel rods. You want more than the fundamentals of electric utility economics? They could deliver that information in their sleep. What they weren't doing well was connecting with their audiences.

> This used-car salesman knew how to connect with his audience…………..Enter Ed Koupal

While Southern California Edison's highly educated and sophisticated professionals were doing their best to win over hearts and pending votes, the opposition was lead by a former used car salesman. Now don't get me wrong, I have nothing against used car sales professionals. But Ed Koupal, who became the communications lightening rod for the People's Lobby, was not the most sophisticated guy on the planet.

I debated Ed before college audiences and on radio. Ed was very good at relating to his audience for one simple reason: He spoke their language. While the engineers talked about the physics of electric energy, good ol' Ed was describing how a brown cloud of nuclear gases would engulf half of Southern California if an accident occurred at the San Onofre Nuclear Generation Station. Ed didn't talk utility economics. Most voters wouldn't understand it. Ed didn't understand it. Most of those going to the polls couldn't care less. The California populous did want to know about the safety of nuclear power reactors. Ed didn't always have his facts correct, but he was on the same wavelength of his audience through his ability to connect emotionally by speaking their language. If The People's Lobby had more Ed Koupals on their side reaching out to voters, Proposition 9 may have passed.

The value of speaking the language of your audience is not limited to the utility industry. A classic example of speaking to the level of your audience was reported in *The Wall Street Journal* Online (WSJ.com) in its August 22, 2005 edition: "In an ominous sign for Merck & Co., it took just an hour for a jury here to blow through the company's principal line of defense: that its painkiller Vioxx couldn't have caused the heart-related death of 59-year-old triathlete Robert Ernst." The WSJ report goes on to say: "But after the first hour or so of deliberation Thursday, a majority of the jury had in effect dispensed with the science and started a series of 10-2 votes against Merck that would end in a $253 million verdict against the drug maker. Interviews with jurors suggest that they tuned out Merck's arguments and focused instead on evidence they understood: that a big corporation allegedly covered up defects with its product.

"Jurors who voted against Merck said much of the science sailed right over their heads. 'Whenever Merck was up there, it was like wah, wah, wah,' said juror John Ostrom, imitating the sounds Charlie Brown's teacher makes in the television cartoon. 'We didn't know what the heck they were talking about.'"

Perhaps the best quotation that captures the essence of speaking the language of the other person comes from former Chrysler Corporation Chairman and business icon Lee Iacocca when he said, "Talk to people in their own language. If you do it well, they'll say, 'God, he said exactly what I was thinking.' And when they begin to respect you, they'll follow you to the death."

Four Communications Styles

Why is it that you can be on one person's communicating "wave length" and not on another's? Have you ever wondered why you get along with one person and not the other? Renowned psychoanalyst Carl Jung and others have articulated the importance of personality and its influence on how people communicate. Jung's work stressed that every individual develops a primacy in one of four major behavioral functions:

Sensing: Doing, competing, striving for results, living in the here and now, and achieving

Thinking: Rationally deducing, analyzing, correlating, weighing options, identifying, and reflecting

Feeling: Empathizing, perceiving; associating, remembering, and relating

Intuiting: Envisioning, creating, inventing, daydreaming, imagining, and speculating

These characteristics reflect themselves in four communicating styles: *Controller, Analyzer, Supporter,* and *Promoter.* There are very few people with "pure styles." According to Dr. Paul P. Mok, psychologist and founder of Training Associates and Training Associates Press of Garland, Texas, each person is endowed with varying degrees of these four primary communications styles, with one of them predominant. An important concept is that we tend to get along better with those whose communication style is similar to our own. Conversely, we have the most difficult time communicating and relating with someone who is in the exact opposite quadrant as ours.

CHAPTER 5 - Taking Personal Communications To The Next Level

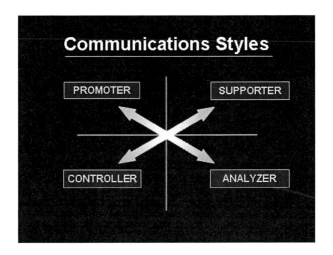

"It means that if I am operating in one style or channel and you are operating in another, then it is likely that we are going to pass each other like ships in the night – silently, without really communicating," Mok says. "It's the sort of thing you feel when you put down the phone, or leave an interview and say to yourself: 'He didn't give me a chance to explain or we just weren't on the same wave length.'"

If you know your own style and if you know the style of the other person, you are much better equipped to communicate in a manner that seems more open and trustworthy to the other person. As communication barriers start to fall, your ability to relate is enhanced because you are more in-sync with each other.

Through your knowledge of communication styles, you are in a position to defuse many communication and personality conflicts. It is important to keep in mind that the study of the four personality types is not an attempt to "pigeon hole" anyone into a specific quadrant, but rather to provide information that will assist a person to align his or her communication with the communication style of the other person. The goal, then, is to assist us to be on the same "wave length" as the other person.

Let's turn attention to a review of the four distinct communications styles so you can determine your style and get a better sense of the style of the challenging person. Once you know your style, we'll review how to determine the style of the other person – even if you are meeting someone for the first time.

Controller – The controller is a doer and often the driving force within an organization. This person leads others. He is the type of person who would say, "Follow me and I will take you to the Promised Land." He is characterized by emphasis on action and results. This person thrives on getting things done here and now. This is the "alpha" dog. Just as the alpha dog must lead the pack, the controller must be first and must lead. He has no time to waste and makes quick decisions. The controller believes in and enjoys only that which is important to him. Controllers tend not to respect an idea until they have personally seen it translated into something practical and doable.

When faced with a new project or task, the controller wants to know *will this work* and *how will this work* and *what is in it for our organization.* This is a bottom line personality. Because he places high standards on himself and others, he is likely to be seen as constructively impatient and tireless. This is the type of person who will give another an opportunity to do a task and if the controller's expectations are not met, he will do the task himself. His attitude is: "Do it right or I'll get it done."

Under stress this person will likely been seen by others as very sensitive to opinions that represent resistance for action. He has a tendency to ignore the feelings of others while failing to assess his impact on others. He can also be seen as opinionated or biased.

Controllers fill occupations that require action and high levels of responsibility. Their careers include CEOs, lawyers, medical doctors, entrepreneurs, pilots, professional athletes, military officers, land developers, construction company owners, bankers, and marketing executives, among others.

How to communicate with the *Controller*:

When communicating or when working with the typical *controller,* be prepared to move fast and to be tested. Expect the controller to argue, interrupt, disagree, raise his voice, and challenge your thoughts. A highly successful law firm partner in Los Angeles said to me one day while we were having a moderately cordial conversation: "Argue with me!" I responded that there really wasn't anything to argue about. Then I realized that was the controller in her. She needed to have an argument – a more accelerated discussion – not for the sake of being belligerent, but to seek out more relevant information.

Keep in mind that this behavior is not an attack on you. The controller's communications is not personal; it is just the way he or she is. You improve your chance for successful communications with this person by getting to the point early on and not flinching when the tone of the discussion accelerates. Show your confidence. Be enthusiastic and assertive. Allow controllers to lead, which they love to do, as they often come equipped with an ample ego.

Analyzer – If you went to Central Casting and asked for a stereotypical analyzer, the person showing up would be wearing the old time green visor and sporting a black armband with a hand crank adding machine. Such is the view many have of the analyzer for he is characterized by analysis, details, logic, and systematic inquiry, and being a bit stiff. This person functions in a steady, tenacious manner, finding great satisfaction in identifying a problem, weighing options carefully, and testing them to determine the best possible solution. The analyzer is not a risk taker.

While not an idea or big picture person, he is seen as a consistent producer who can handle pressure. He is often valued for his thoughtful analysis rather than for his skill in mobilizing or leading others. The analyzer is of great value as a logical thinker who provides objectivity to a complex problem. Another strength of the analyzer is his capacity to handle pressure. When others may have their thinking adversely affected by the pressures of the day, this person remains calm and focused. Don't expect him to be the life of the party, but he will show up on time!

A weakness of the analyzer is the tendency to be overly cautious, at the expense of making timely decisions. Seemingly in need of more data prior to reaching a decision, he can be a stumbling block to taking action. In his biography, former Chrysler Chairman Lee Iacocca, references this type of personality saying that Chrysler had too many analyzers always in need of more information before making decisions, which contributed to missed marketing opportunities. "I have always found that if I move with seventy-five percent or more of the facts that I usually never regret it. It's the guys who wait to have everything perfect that drive you crazy," Iacocca states.

Occupations of the analyzer include lawyers, engineers, accountants, financial planners, technicians, professors, scientists, executive directors of law and accounting firms, systems analysts, data processors, and science and math teachers, to name a few.

How to communicate with the *Analyzer*:
When communicating with or when working with analyzers, be well organized, have details lined up, and plan each meeting carefully. Discuss the agenda prior to any meetings. Speak slowly as he processes information more carefully than most. Ameliorate via explanation. Pause as you speak with him and ask questions to make sure you are both on the same page of your topic of discussion.

One of the surest means for creating a communication barrier with the analyzer is to generalize. Keeping in mind that this person is very detailed in thought and in discussion, you need to guard against speaking in general terms. Think specifics when communicating with the analyzer.

Supporter – A concern for people dominates the thinking and behavior of the *supporter* style. His concern for people and an understanding of them provides the supporter with an uncanny ability to "read" people and to be "tuned" into an organization's rumor mill. While messages created by office politics often go right by many, very little gets by the supporter. He is really tuned in to what is unsaid in an organization. He is often sought out for his ability to empathize and for his patience with others during a time of crisis.

An understanding listener, he can identify change in ways that reduce conflicting forces and increase the likelihood of cooperation and teamwork. However, he does have a shortcoming or two. A weakness among supporters is their tendency to become emotional, which may be viewed as a substitution for taking action. Under pressure, he may be seen as thin-skinned or over-reactive.

Of the four personality types, the supporter is the most likely to flinch – to back away – in a time of conflict. Don't rely exclusively on this person to support you in a time of crisis. While he may have the best of intentions to be of assistance, the supporter is not likely to be the strong-willed individual you desire in a time of need.

Typical supporters include human resource and personnel professionals, teachers, public relations professionals, nurses, clergy, athletic coaches, receptionists, social service workers, writers, psychologists, psychiatrists, retail employees, and individuals in real estate, among others.

How to communicate with the *Supporter*:

Effective communication with the supporter is best achieved through an informal, open and personalized approach. Of the four communication styles, the supporter, more than others, makes time available to talk. If you ask how much time he has to meet and discuss an issue, his response is likely to be whatever time you need. Express your enthusiasm when communicating with the supporter and feel free to explain why the issue is personally important to you. After all, this is a people-oriented person with whom you are communicating.

Because the supporter is often seen as being thin-skinned and overly sensitive, your face-to-face communications should be somewhat guarded. Maintain ample physical space between yourself and the supporter type. While you can be enthusiastic, even somewhat aggressive when communicating with the *controller*, the *supporter* will balk at signs of aggressive communications.

Promoter – The big picture person has just arrived. The promoter style is characterized by heavy emphasis on ideas, innovation, concepts, and long-range thinking. Imagination is a dominant characteristic of this style. The promoter will challenge you – not because she is hostile – but because she has learned the value of constant probing to uncover new ideas.

A fast and deep thinker, she questions herself and others. She is not inclined to take things for granted. The promoter is seen as a leader and a visionary capable of seeing new possibilities that others do not sense. This person can be impatient and irritated with others who seek detailed evidence or do not see the value of the promoter's ideas. This is a person with a strong ego who can come across as "superior" and can be condescending in her communications. Quick thinking and a quick wit are characteristics of the promoter.

How to communicate with the *Promoter*:

When communicating with the promoter, probe for her ideas and concepts. Ask questions of this person. Because so much of this individual's ego is invested in what she does and how she does it, communicate your awareness of her ideas, plans, and most of all, her vision. Feel free to ask questions of this person's views. She normally loves to talk about her views on issues she thinks are important.

Shortly after takeoff on a flight from Los Angeles to the United Kingdom, I asked the gentleman seated next to me what business he was in. I believe he finished telling me about his trucking and storage business when we were somewhere over Greenland! People – especially promoters – love to talk about their vision and their business. Lucky for me that I hadn't decided to take a nap because he described his relationship with a law firm that was the very same firm I was to meet with two days later in Glasgow, Scotland. I was able to enter that meeting armed with meaningful information about one of that law firm's very own clients thanks to the promoter sitting next to me on that flight.

Promoters love to talk about their plans. Let them have at it. Sit back and absorb.

For a clue to your communicating style, complete "An Experiment in Communications Styles" (Exhibit 5).

Exhibit 5

An Experiment in Communications Styles

Each self-descriptive statement has four endings. Write the number **4** on the line before the completed statement that best describes you. Insert **3** before the ending that is next most like you; **2** before the next most; and **1** before the completed statement that is least descriptive of you.

I am likely to impress others as:

____ A. Practical and to the point
____ B. Emotional and somewhat stimulating
____ C. Astute and logical
____ D. Intellectually oriented and somewhat complex

When confronted by others with a different point of view, I can usually make progress by:

____ A. Getting at least one or two specific commitments on which we can "build" later
____ B. Trying to place myself in the "shoes" of the other person
____ C. Keeping my composure and helping others to see things simply and logically
____ D. Relying on my basic ability to conceptualize and pull ideas together

I feel satisfied with myself when I:

____ A. Get more definite things accomplished than I planned
____ B. Comprehend the underlying feeling of others and react in a helpful way
____ C. Solve a problem by using a logical or systematic method
____ D. Develop new thoughts or ideas that can be related

Add all numbers in the "A" boxes, **(Controller)**. Add numbers in the "B" boxes **(Supporter)**; "C" boxes **(Analyzer)**; and "D" boxes **(Promoter)**. The highest score indicates your primary Communications Style, with the second highest score your backup or your secondary score.

To obtain a sense of how you can use this information to improve communicating with the challenging person, think of how that person would respond to each of these questions.

An Experiment in Communications Styles – based on *The Communicating Styles Survey* copyrighted by Dr. Paul P. Mok, available at Training Associates Press, Garland, TX. www.tapress.com

CHAPTER 5 - Taking Personal Communications To The Next Level

So how do we determine where the challenging person falls? We're not likely to ask him to take a test to find out, and we don't need to do that. Just reflect on the information we have just covered and think about the quadrant where you believe he or she is located. Still not certain? Not to fret. *"Behavioral Styles Overview"* (Exhibit 5.1) will help you to further identify your style and that of the other person.

There are additional ways to get a sense of a person's communication style. For example, the condition of a person's office or desk is one clue. Is the person's desk tidy and neat? Is paper strewn about? Does this person's office have photos of family, sports figures, or does it have high-priced art?

I once worked closely with a partner of a large United States law firm who had flown numerous sorties during the Viet Nam war. His office included photos of his naval pilot experience. There were photos of him seated in the cockpit. There were photos of him standing next to his prized fighter jet. Which of the four styles do you think he matched? If you chose *controller*, you're right on target. It makes sense for a fighter pilot to be a controller. When you put your life and the lives of others on the line, you had better be in control. His legal specialty was – not a surprise – litigator.

Exhibit 5.1

Characteristics	Controller	Analyzer	Supporter	Promoter
Work-Space:	Busy, Formal, Efficient, Structured	Structured, Organized Functional, Formal	Personal, Relaxed, Friendly, Informal	Stimulating, Personal Cluttered, Friendly
Appearance:	Businesslike, Functional	Formal, Conservative	Casual, Comforting	Fashionable, Stylish
Behavioral Focus	Doing, Competing, Getting Results	Structure, Logic, Organization, Problem-solving	Expressive, Human Interaction, Projects Feelings	Imagination, Envisioning, Speculation
Value Orientation	Action, Winning, Wealth	Quality, Being Right, Ethics	Family, Friendship, Loyalty	Concepts, Ideology, Discovery
Seeks:	Productivity	Accuracy	Attention	Recognition
Motivated by:	Stimulating Action, Achievement, Controlling, Gaining an Edge	Logical, Scientific Challenge, Systematic Inquiry	Love, Sense of Contribution, Recognition	Pioneering Spirit, Inventing, Creating
Needs to Know Benefits:	What it Does, By When, What it Costs	How to Justify the Purchase Logically, How it Works	How it will Affect His or Her Personal Circumstances	How it will enhance His or Her Status, Who Else Does it
Fears:	Loss of Control	Embarrassment	Confrontation	Loss of Prestige
Hobby Orientation	Competitive Sports, Wheeling-Dealing, Acquiring, Gambling, Finance Publications, Action Games	Non-fiction Books, Computers, Photography, Collecting	Social, Entertaining, Family Interaction, Volunteering, Beach Scene	Reading, Walking, Back-packing, Chess, Intellectual Games
Oral Communication	Assertive, Controlling, Confronting	Structured, Careful	Personalized, Marked Voice Inflection	Stream of Consciousness
Written Communication	Short, Simple, Directed to Action	Planned, Organized, Geometric	Unplanned, Spontaneous, Warm	Technically Oriented, Idea-Oriented
Likes You to Be:	To the Point	Precise	Pleasant	Stimulating
Dress Preference	Functional	Conservative	Informal	Unpredictable

Characteristics	Controller	Analyzer	Supporter	Promoter
Work Environment Preference:	Demanding, Fast-Paced, Competitive	Ordered, Neat, Data at Hand	Homey, Comfortable	Think-Tank, High-Tech
Wants to Be:	In Charge	Correct	Liked	Admired
Irritated by	Inefficiency, Indecision	Surprises, Unpredictability	Insensitivity	Inflexibility, Routine
Priority:	Results	The Process	Relationships, Interacting	Maintaining Relationships
Under Tension	Dictate/Assert	Withdraw/Avoid	Submit Acquiesce	Attacks, Be Sarcastic
Decisions Are	Definite	Deliberate	Considered	Spontaneous

Behavioral Styles Overview -- Copyright Dr. Paul P. Mok, All rights reserved-Not to be reproduced without express permission of Dr. Mok, Training Associates Press, Garland, TX. www.tapress.com

Of the 2,000 lawyers I have tested in seven countries, 85 percent fall into the *controller* or *analyzer* style. If you are about to communicate with a controller – not to mention an ex-fighter pilot – have your act together and get to the point!

Another way to obtain a sense of a person's communications style is by assessing the way the person talks on the phone or communicates in writing. Here are some indicators to help identify a person's communications style:

During telephone conversations:
    Controller – Quick, to the point, controls conversation
    Analyzer – Specific, detailed, ordered, measured
    Supporter – Amicable, friendly, warm-hearted
    Promoter – Cool, distant, impersonal

Written communications:
    Controller – To the point, action driven, urgent

Analyzer – Structured, formal, rigid, specific

Supporter – Private, personalized, subjective

Promoter – Hypothetical, ideal, intellectual

Let's Summarize…………..
Controller
- Is in charge and wants results
- Is driven by facts, logic, and reason
- Is self-confident, independent, and strong willed
- Expects others to work as hard as he/she does
- Does not waste time
- Is impatient
- Knows things will get done when he is in control
- Is fast-paced and task oriented
- Takes charge in unfamiliar situations
- Thinks quickly, makes decisions with whatever facts are available

Analyzer
- Is a logical results-getter
- Is not a visionary or idea person
- Is consistent
- Is a methodical worker
- Is good with numbers, analyses, and processes
- Enjoys problem solving

- Enjoys working alone
- Is diplomatic
- Is oriented to the present
- Is short on giving praise
- Normally, does not hurt other's feelings

Supporter
- Is enthusiastic
- Is friendly
- Is talkative
- Is optimistic
- Is lacking in concept of time
- Is generally, not good with numbers – not analytical
- Is a people person - possesses strong concern for people and an understanding of them
- Is sought out by individuals for his/her ability to listen, empathize, and for patience in assisting others experiencing troubles or crisis in their lives

Promoter
- Is a visionary
- Is imaginative
- Is creative
- Emphasizes ideas, innovation concepts, theory, and long-range planning

- Questions herself and others
- Challenges others because he/she has learned the value of continuous probing

Word Choices That Stimulate Positive Responses

Each communication style responds differently to different words. Here are a few words that normally stimulate positive responses. Use these words to enhance communications with the challenging personality:

Controller	**Analyzer**
Planned	*Experience*
Completed	*Factual*
Mission	*Proven*
Objective	*Principles*
Return on investment	
Competitive advantage	

Supporter	**Promoter**
Consensus	*Possible*
Flexible	*Doable*
Adaptable	*Hunches*
Reliable	*Innovative*
Dependable	*Ingenious*
Precedent	

Chapter 6 - Building The All-Important Rapport

> *"Louis, I think this is the beginning of a beautiful friendship."*
>
> Rick Blaine
> *Casablanca* (1942)

Would it not benefit you and the challenging person to create a communications relationship that goes beyond merely resolving your differences? If you can improve your communications with this person – and you can by applying the body of knowledge we have discussed to this point – why can't you take your communications to a higher plane? Think about it. You don't have to become bosom buddies with the other person, but as long as you're investing time with him or her – at work; on a committee; in a social environment – why not get the most out of this communications experience? Be selfish for a moment. Remember the WIIFM (What's In It For Me?). There's your answer. Don't settle for just resolving a personal communications problem with this guy. Get the most you can from this encounter and tuck away the experience into your work/life resume. You can call on this experience as your career continues to advance.

Being able to inform senior level management of your ability to solve communications problems and to strengthen relationships with a problem person is a valued resource in any organization. Your goal should be more than solving a communications challenge. Your goal is to establish rapport and trust with this person. Let's see how we can make this happen.

> Rapport is to relationships as fuel is to a car.

First, let's get an understanding of just what is meant by rapport. Rapport is a relationship with another person based on understanding, emotional infinity, and mutual trust. Rapport creates the probability of relating well with another person. If we relate well with another person, we increase the prospects that others will agree with us or at least they will see things from our point of view.

In *Instant Rapport,* author Michael Brooks points out that rapport is experiencing the world through the same portal as the person with whom you are communicating. "It's speaking the same language, even when you don't necessarily understand each other's words," Brooks says. "It's truly being able to make others' points of view your own and having them accept your point of view as their own. It's traveling down the same road."

Let me introduce you to the four pillars upon which rapport is created: *Interest, Understanding, Trust, and Humility.*

Interest – Building rapport through *interest* means finding the curiosity within yourself to want to learn about the other person. Your goal at this point is to understand who the person is rather than what the person represents. Take the initiative to learn about the other person so you can more easily identify common ground. Take your curiosity temperature. Are you curious enough to identify elements of common ground with the difficult person? If not, you are at a disadvantage in your efforts to communicate and to cope with the other person. Be curious enough to determine something about his likes and his dislikes. Does he enjoy talking about politics, sports, which teams? Start your conversation with this person knowing what he likes and avoid his dislikes. Be curious as curiosity unlocks the doors to finding real interest in the other person. By completing the form "<u>Key Information for Creating Rapport</u>" (Exhibit 6) at the end of this chapter, you will have enough meaningful information to initiate and to maintain dialogue with the challenging person. Sources for this information range from the person's secretary, the person's colleagues, and industry members to *People Search* and *Net Detective* on the Internet. As your dialogue expands, your opportunities to establish rapport with this person significantly increase.

Remember Herb, the guy who gave my staff and me all the grief we could want? If I had sought common ground with him, our relationship and our communications most likely would have taken on a different, more favorable tone. Had I demonstrated more curiosity back then and learned more about him, I would have been privy to information valuable to our relationship. I failed to do that and that was my shortcoming.

For example, he was in his 50's and was father to a young daughter whom he adored. So what's the value of that information? His residence was in San Diego, California, but his office and work were based in Los Angeles. This meant, among other things, that he was away from his daughter much of the week. How simple it would have been for me to seek an opportunity to bring up the joy he must get when he and his daughter are together and how much of a challenge it could be for him to be away from her for days at a time. Although I was newly married and had no children at that time, I could have found common ground with him through his daughter. All I would have had to do was reference how close my family was and how my father was never away one night from us children. Seeking common ground was my responsibility and I failed to do that with my difficult and challenging construction industry colleague.

"You get along better with people when the emphasis is on similarities between you," say authors Brinkman and Kirschner in *Dealing With People You Can't Stand*. "The difference between conflict with a friend and conflict with a difficult person, is that with a friend the conflict is tempered by the common ground you share. Success in communications depends on finding common ground before attempting to redirect the interaction toward a new outcome."

Understanding – Interest gets us through the door of the other person. Now we have to see what is inside the room. Seek to learn what makes this person unique by asking insightful questions accompanied by astute listening. Wanting to know about the other person and what he or she thinks will unearth valuable insight into this individual. Ask open-ended questions of this person and be quiet. One of the best ways to demonstrate your interest in the other person so that you can acquire the needed understanding is to not speak, but to listen and observe the non-verbal cues he or she gives off. Consider their tone of voice, their body language, gestures, and their attitude as they respond to your questions. Seek to learn the true meaning behind words and body movement. If we listen only to words or observe only body language, we risk receiving partial communications. The objective when seeking a real understanding of the other person is to absorb all of the communications he can provide.

In *The 7 Habits of Highly Effective People*, author Stephen Covey points out that the greatest need of human beings – after physical survival – is to be understood, affirmed, validated, and appreciated. He comments that empathetic listening gets inside another person's frame of reference. You look out through it, you see the world the way they see the world, you understand their paradigm, you understand how they feel. If we can start to understand how the challenging person feels about an issue of concern to us, then we are on our way to creating the rapport so vital to enhancing our relationship.

Trust – When seeking a definition of the third pillar of rapport – trust – I turned to a friend, Steven R. Loranger, chairman and chief executive officer of ITT Industries. Steve so aptly defines trust this way: "Trust means creating a relationship grounded on one's ability to feel comfortable that the other person is indeed a partner, working to a common goal to create a success that both parties can effect, in a greater way than each could individually."

There is a certain risk in trusting someone, especially if he or she is a real challenge to be around. Becoming vulnerable is part of trust building. You may be hurt by the other person if he knows your weaknesses and your strengths, but this is an essential step in trust-building. If you are to create change for the better with the challenging personality, take the risk. You will find it to be worth the reward.

Humility – While setting aside one's ego to concentrate attention and energy on the other person is not only a challenge for most people, it is a key to creating rapport. By leaving our ego at the door, we eliminate a major barrier to relating to the challenging person. To effectively communicate with the difficult individual, we must shed ourselves of biases and emotions. Taking on a posture of humility allows us to do just that. As Father George O'Brien, Ph.D., a close friend and a professor at Mount Saint Mary's College in Brentwood, California, says: "Humility may not be fashionable in the business world, but I am convinced that humility in companies would improve balance sheets."

Considering the number of scandals at the highest levels of supposed corporate leadership in the U.S., do you think out-of-control ego may have contributed to these leaders' demise? As a possible answer to that question, I call upon Saint Thomas Aquinas who so aptly stated: "Humility is truth."

Exhibit 6

KEY INFORMATION FOR CREATING RAPPORT
Use this form to create improved relationships with others

HOMETOWN _____
High School_____Year Graduated____
College/University_____Year Graduated____
   Fraternity/Sorority_____
   College sports:_____
   Extra-curricular activities: _____
Is higher education a sensitive issue? _____
Trade School _____ Specialty_____
Military service:_____Discharge rank:_____
Union member:_____Offices held:_____
Honors received:_____
What do you believe is this person's greatest concern regarding his job/career responsibilities? _____
Is this a powerful individual within his/her organization?____
   Who influences his/her position of authority?_____
Spouse _____Anniversary Date_____
   Hometown:_____Education:_____
   Interests:_____
Children ___ Names/Ages _____
Clubs/Organizations/Offices _____
Political party_____Active?_____
Religion:_____Active?_____
Hobbies:_____
What is his long-term personal objective? (this may be personal or career/business related):_____
What is his immediate objective? (this may be personal or career/business related): _____
How does this person want to be remembered within his organization _____

Chapter 7 – Eight Activities To Improve Personal Relations

> *"Never tell people how to do things. Tell them what to do and they will surprise you with their ingenuity."*
> General George S. Patton, Jr.
> *Patton* (1970)

To this point we have been focusing on how to communicate more effectively with difficult people. But we know that life in general and our working environment in particular are not simple. Not only do we have to communicate with them; we have to work with them. Most of the people you will encounter at work are enjoyable to be around. However, there are always a few that can challenge one's patience. These twits come in all sizes and shapes and they bring a variety of baggage with them – bad attitudes, egos, paranoia. Some of these folks talk constantly and never listen. Others must have the last word. While some criticize to a person's face; others snipe behind your back. Regardless of their behavior, one thing is certain: You have to deal with them. You have to cope with them. You cannot ignore them hoping they will miraculously change for the better. It isn't going to happen.

Left unaddressed, your situation will not get any better – it is highly likely to get worse. You may also be viewed as a difficult person who is unable to remedy a problem situation. In addition, problem relationships that linger can result in your being labeled high maintenance, not a career-enhancing reputation to have. So what can be done to change your relationship with the challenging person for the better? Here are eight activities to help us do just that.

1. *Modify your attitude*: Let's examine our attitude towards resolving challenges presented by the difficult person. If I do not have the desire to resolve differences with that person, how can I expect positive change? W. Clement Stone was one of America's most successful business professionals. In the late 1920's Stone built the Combined Insurance Company of America, and by 1930 he had over 1000 agents selling insurance for him across the United States. By 1979 Stone's insurance company exceeded $1 billion in assets. His company merged with the Patrick Ryan Group to form the *Aon Corporation* in 1987. *Combined Insurance Company* is one of *Aon's* largest subsidiaries. Stone was a best selling author. In 1960, he teamed up with Napoleon Hill to author *Success Through a Positive Mental Attitude*. Above all, Stone emphasized using a "positive mental attitude" to make money for himself, and for millions of people who read his

books. He re-emphasizes the value of one's attitude when he says: "There is little difference in people. The little difference is a big difference. The little difference is attitude. The big difference is whether one attitude is positive or negative." Our attitude drives our behavior. Our attitude either ignites or stifles our enthusiasm to make things better. The importance of one's attitude in creating a better relationship with another person can never be undervalued.

We can also learn from Viktor Frankl something of great value regarding attitude. Viktor Frankl was born in Vienna in 1905 and graduated with two doctorates in Medicine and Philosophy from the University of Vienna. In September of 1942, the young doctor, his new bride, his mother, father, and brother, were arrested in Vienna and taken to a concentration camp in Bohemia. His father died there of starvation. His mother and brother were killed in Auschwitz in 1944. His wife died at Bergen-Belsen in 1945. It was events that occurred there and at three other camps that led the young doctor – prisoner 119,104 – to realize the significance of meaningfulness in life.

Among Frankl's most poignant notations is the following: "We who lived in concentration camps can remember the men who walked through the huts comforting others, giving away their last piece of bread. They may have been few in number, but they offer sufficient proof that everything can be taken from a man but one thing: The last of the human freedoms – to choose one's attitude in any given set of circumstances."

Frankl also wrote how he used his attitude as a source of strength to get him through the most grueling circumstances. He has noted how he would stand looking beyond the fence and the wire that bound those inside the camp. By using his attitude he would think of what life would be like when he would be free. If attitude can play such a pivotal role in a person's life under these incredible conditions, then we should be able to utilize our attitude to successfully cope with difficult and challenging personalities in our daily lives.

In April of 1945, Frankl's camp was liberated, and he returned to Vienna, only to discover the deaths of his loved ones. Although nearly broken and very much alone in the world, he was given the position of director of the Vienna Neurological Policlinic – a position he would hold for 25 years. In the 1960's he moved to the United States. He held visiting professorships at Harvard and other U.S. universities, and did over 50 American lecture tours. Viktor Frankl died in the same week as Mother Teresa and Princess Diana in 1997.

Our previous encounters with challenging people mold our attitude towards them. To create change for the better, we must establish a more open and pristine attitude. We cannot maintain the same attitude towards this person and expect positive change on our part, let alone on his. As that noted philosopher, Yogi Berra so eloquently put it: "If you do what you've always done, you're gonna get what you always got." Any change in our behavior is generated through a change in our attitude.

2. *Let go of your agenda*: With a favorable attitude for change serving as the foundation for action, our second activity is to let go of our agenda. Set aide feelings of frustration, disappointment, ill-will, or anger lingering from your experience with this person. Let them go. This can be very difficult for some of us. After all, the challenging person can create pain for you and for your co-workers. However, a clean slate is needed. Empty yourself of any pre-conceived ideas, assumptions or expectations – anything that might twist what you will hear into something other than what was meant.

3. *Make an ally*: One goal is to create or to reinforce trust with this person. To gain this trust, think of the other person as a friend. Now you're probably thinking: "Why should I give a hoot about turning this person into an ally of mine? I can't stand the jerk!" Remember the good ol' WIIFM? Unless you can avoid this person, then it is in your best interests to make him into a friend. If this person is your boss, your career interests are at stake. If this person is a co-worker who you can't avoid, your piece of

mind is at stake. By *friend*, I am not suggesting that you spend hours socializing together. I am recommending that you come to grips with the reality of personal relationships.

Let me give you an example. Jack was a senior associate at an international law firm based in Los Angeles. He was bright. He was a good technical lawyer who spoke several languages. He said to me one day: "Do you know how much time I spend with our firm lawyers after work?" He answered his own question by forming a zero with his index finger and thumb. Associate lawyers in law firms attend some of the best law schools in the country. They work hard and long hours. They can invest up to eight years with the hopes of making partner. The stakes are high. Firm partners vote on which associates do or do not make partner. For whatever it is worth, Jack didn't make partner. Sometimes you just have to change your attitude to generate the results you want.

Here are sample phrases that will assist communicating with the other person. Note, you are not agreeing with this potential ally. You are merely clarifying and conveying interest in what has been said:

> *"Let me build on that and see if we are on the same track."*
>
> *"May I support what you are saying with another point?"*

4. *Empathize*: Empathy is a powerful means for resolving conflicts and for reinforcing trust. A rule to follow: *Speak and act as though you were the one about to hear what you are poised to say or to experience what you plan to do.* Use these types of statements when appropriate:

- *"I understand why you feel that way."*
- *"I understand."*

Needless to say, you should not state that you know exactly how the other person feels for one obvious reason: You can't know exactly how he feels. By recalling similar experiences you may come close, but you cannot know precisely how that person interprets or reacts to circumstances similar to yours. To state so would do more damage than good for your relationship. Even when two people have experienced the same event, their mental images of that event will not be identical.

5. *Seek feedback*: Our fifth activity is to solicit feedback during communications. Feedback helps the person who is talking to feel heard and appreciated. This is not the same as agreeing or disagreeing with what this person has said. Effective feedback provides an opportunity to confirm, correct, or improve your understanding of the other person's communications.

All too often individuals claim to be interested in what the other person has to say, only to feign legitimate interest. By seeking feedback you are demonstrating – not talking the proverbial talk, but walking the walk – your interest in what the other person is saying. Try these statements when communicating with your challenging person:

- *"Let me see if I understand what you just said."* [Summarize in your own words that which you believe you have heard.]
- *"Is that correct?"*

6. *Ask open-ended questions*: If we want to demonstrate a sincere interest in what the other person is saying, then what better way to do that than asking for his opinion? One of the best ways to secure valuable feedback is to ask questions that cannot be answered *yes* or *no*. People love to give their opinions. They just don't want to be interrupted with public opinion surveying via telephone calls during dinner! Here are a few suggested questions:

- *"I would like your opinion. How might we resolve this issue?"*
- *"What do you think the best solution might be?"*
- *"Will you please tell me more about that?"*

- *"In your opinion, what is the best way to proceed?"*

7. *Search behind the words:* After you empty yourself of your judgments, listen to the words used by the other person. Much is communicated beyond the words themselves. Try to identify the deeper issues and hear assumptions, expectations, and hidden meanings that lie beneath what is being said. You will learn a great deal more than others who ignore the subsurface of communications. You will also communicate to the other person that what he is saying is important to you.

8. *Recognize contribution*: Everyone likes to be appreciated. Thank the person for communicating with you. Once again, you do not have to agree with the other person. You can enhance your relationship with the other person by stating that you value the opportunity to discuss issues that are important to you. You might say something liked the following:

- *"I have found our time together meaningful."*
- *"I learned a great deal from what you just said, specifically* [state exactly what you learned from this person]."
- *"I realize you are busy and I want you to know that I appreciated our conversation."*

Expand the above list of questions to include those that you feel comfortable asking the other person. Remember, if change for the better is to occur, your attitude will be the driving force for that change.

Chapter 8 – Coping With The Difficult Boss

> *"I'm too tired to scream from the pain you just caused me."*
> Elliott
> *He Knows You're Alone* (1980)

Difficult bosses are a big problem. Bad bosses can frustrate you, irritate you, demotivate you. They may be authoritarian, paranoid, introverted, extroverted, aggressive, passive, control freaks, bullies, self-absorbed or a combination of these. Their behavior can keep you on edge, not knowing what they may do next. They can play favorites, giving praise and support to lesser deserving individuals. Some bosses love to make you feel insecure in your future, and, if left unchecked, they can ruin your career. Whatever form they take, the impact bosses can have on the work environment ranges from highly enjoyable to astutely dreadful.

The number one reason employees quit their jobs, according to a Gallup poll of more than one million U.S. employees, is their boss. The poll also concludes that the length of time employees stay at companies and how productive they are is determined by their relationship with their immediate supervisor. When employees leave due to problem relationships with their boss, both the employee and the company can suffer. Employees suffer because they have sincerely wanted to establish a meaningful and productive career with their employer. Organizations can suffer because productivity declines and good employees leave taking with them valuable experience and intellectual resources that cannot be replaced overnight.

A Saratoga Institute study, based on interviews with 20,000 employees who had recently left an employer, revealed that the main reason people quit is the manager's behavior. So what are some of the characteristics of these bosses who earn the dubious moniker of P-I-T-S (pain-in-the-shorts)? Any of these sound familiar?

The Boss:
    Can never be satisfied
    Does not stand up for employees
    Believes employees are fungible
    Offers little or no recognition for employees' hard work
    Does not trust employees
    Provides little or no meaningful direction
    Plays favorites among employees
    Does not really respect employees
    Does not give meaningful feedback

Avoids discussing face-to-face issues of importance
Does not involve employees in tough processes
Can be rude to employees
Enjoys intimidating employees
Talks, but doesn't support work/family balance
Gives too many tasks with impossible deadlines
Is an ineffective communicator
Is not someone with whom you want to spend free time

There is some bad news and some good news regarding difficult bosses. First, the bad news. Difficult bosses have been around a long time and they aren't going away any time soon. Today, however, we're seeing more bad bosses than ever before. As a result of institutionalized leanness, overextended managers are both short-tempered and too busy or ill-trained to provide staff with the support they need. According to research from Denver, Colorado career coach Gordon Miller, eighty-one percent of 700 employees surveyed classified their immediate supervisor as a "lousy manager," up a third from sixty-three percent just two years prior. Another sixty-nine percent said their boss had "no clue" on what to do to become a "good manager." No one has as much power as a difficult boss to unnerve employees and damage their sense of self-esteem. This is why it is understood more often than not, that people don't quit jobs, they quit bosses.

The authors of *Primal Leadership* state that "Roughly 50 to 70 percent of how employees perceive their organizational climate can be traced to the actions of one person: the leader. More than anyone else, the boss creates the conditions that determine people's ability to work well." Indeed, growing evidence suggests that leaders make a difference. The issue at stake is what kind of difference does your boss make? Some bosses inspire others to greatness. Some bosses drive good people out the door.

"In today's rapidly changing work life, perceived justice in the form of effective leadership practices, participative management and emotionally intelligent bosses has become increasingly important to employees," says Kenneth Nowack, Ph.D., President and Chief Research Officer of Envisia Learning of Santa Monica, California. "Employees who work for "competent jerks" are significantly more likely to be actively disengaged, experience more job stress and absenteeism due to physical illness and less likely to remain committed to the organization. Indeed, the interpersonal competence of leaders may be one of the most strategic competitive advantages that an organization can leverage for long-term success."

Leadership practices are intimately linked to diverse measures of organizational success. A recent study by *Envisia Learning* provided support for the hypothesis that leadership effectiveness, defined as involvement-oriented and sensitive management practices, can have a significant impact on an employee's commitment, perceptions of stress and retention. Employees who rated leaders in the organization as effective were less likely to consider leaving within 12 months, were more engaged and satisfied with work and reported significantly less stress compared to those who rated leadership practices as less effective overall.

Having competent bosses is not only good for employee relationships; it is good for business. *Envisia Learning* further reports that a meta-analysis of over 7,900 business units in 38 companies explored the relationship at the business-unit level between employee satisfaction-engagement and the business-unit outcomes of customer satisfaction, productivity, profit, employee turnover, and accidents (Harter & Schmidt, 2002). Generalizable relationships, large enough to have substantial practical value, were found between unit-level employee satisfaction-engagement and these business-unit outcomes suggesting that management practices that affect satisfaction can have bottom line results on productivity and profit.

Ok, we know that some people make just bad bosses. So how do they end up in such positions of authority? The answer: Bosses become bosses for a variety of reasons. Those who become bosses may or may not be ideal boss material. They don't always have the skills necessary to be an effective manager of people, yet they are given positions of authority over projects and, more importantly, over people. Let's look at some of the reasons certain individuals are elevated to bossdom.

Technical Expertise – A person who has consistently proven to have expert knowledge often is looked upon as a leader. People pay attention to this person when he or she speaks. A certain amount of respect is granted – and rightly so – to these people. They can separate themselves from the pack through the depth and breadth of their technical knowledge. Unfortunately, technical expertise does not necessarily transfer to the skills of an effective manager. Professional service firms are notorious for assigning management and other leadership positions to partners who have little, if any, management and supervisory education.

> *"I eliminated them because they had a typo!"*

I was asked to produce a short list of public relations firms that I felt were qualified to provide certain services to a large U.S.-based law firm. Having served as Regional Manager for the Southwest office of then the world's third largest PR firm, I felt confident that I could identify several qualified candidates. After identifying three PR firms – all capable of doing quality work – I turned the interview process over to the partner in charge of marketing for the law firm. Each PR firm then made a capabilities presentation to the partner. When I inquired with the partner how the interviews went, she informed me that she eliminated one of the three firms because they had a typographical error in their presentation. I think we would all agree that professionals should not have typos in their presentations. However, while her intentions were honorable, she failed to think like an executive and more like a lawyer reviewing the draft of a contract. That mindset produced another result: The firm she eliminated, I believe, would have done the best job for that law firm.

Companies that survey managers and employees often find that well over half (often 75 percent or more) of managers surveyed felt they did not have the information or interpersonal communication skills they needed to make their staff members as productive as possible or meet their staff members needs for critical information. Similar percentages of employees felt they did not have the information they needed on the goals of the company, the company's business, their roles in meeting company goals, etc. to contribute to the company the way they were able and willing to do.

I mentioned to the Managing Partner of the largest UK office of one of the largest firms in the legal profession that he could become chairman of that firm some day. His response was that he was not ready. When I asked him why he felt that way he replied "I'm a lawyer. I don't have the necessary management skills." I compiled a list of short management courses taught at some of the premiere universities in the U.S. Since then he has completed courses at Harvard and the Wharton School of Business at the University of Pennsylvania. To his credit he recognized business and management skills shortcomings and he did something about them. He later became one of three finalists for chairman of that firm. Had he not withdrawn his name – for personal reasons – I am convinced he would have been elected chairman of that international firm. It is not mandatory to attend Harvard or Wharton. What is needed among many of those with leadership titles is to honestly assess their leadership and management skills and acquire the knowledge needed to help them to achieve leadership success.

Success – People are promoted to management because they are successful. They get things done. If they are in sales, they bring in the numbers. If they are in advertising, they are great at creating. If they are in journalism, they have a great nose for the next major news story. If they are in architecture, they excel at designing things. You get the picture. You can bring in the numbers; you can create; you can design, and still not be an effective boss. None of these positions guarantees anyone will be an effective boss.

Seniority – If a person has been around long enough, he is likely at some point in his career to be in a position of authority. Sometimes the most inept find themselves with power over others because they have been around longer than anyone else. They have seen management come and go. They have survived the political battles. They have survived cutbacks and layoffs. They have avoided conflict because they have been astute at knowing risks to take and risks to avoid. If they bring unique skills to the work environment it is their political acumen. They know who to embrace and who to avoid. They are survivors. They are, unfortunately, responsible for others and few of their survival skills have prepared them to effectively manage others.

Political Reasons – Having community clout is another reason certain individuals are promoted to bossdom. Being well known within an industry or within a geographical community can spearhead one to a position of leadership. This is certainly true among many professional service firms. The person holding the title *Senior Partner* is a person of great influence within the service firm. The title of Senior Partner is bestowed on a firm member who has proven his or her technical competence and is well known and normally highly regarded among community leaders. This person generates new business. She is very good at relating well with others. She is highly positioned on several civic boards. She is in a position of authority because she knows how to move among community decision makers. While being politically connected can serve many purposes, it does not ensure managerial competence.

Four Types of Difficult Bosses

While we could identify many different types of bad bosses – from the super possessive to super aggressive from the obsessive micro-manager to the political animal – by reviewing the following four types, we will have covered many of the issues that employees face with their challenging bosses.

Super Ego – One of the more prevalent types of bosses possessing an inherent capability to irritate others and make the working environment all the more challenging is the *Super Ego*. While normally bright and extremely driven, this boss is a legend in his own mind. Arrogance, lack of empathy for others, and a limited conscience are personality traits found in this type of boss. He is friendly and charming to those who can do something of value for him. While having an ego can be beneficial – I have never met a successful person who lacked some degree of egotism – this boss is a master manipulator. In his mind, no one can do the job quite as well as he can.

Ego-driven bosses promote those who flatter them and are hostile to those who do not. He focuses on finding the flaw in everything you do. Proving a person's shortcomings makes his day. Seeking out the activities of others that he can criticize reinforces in his mind his value as a boss. His persona can be summarized as follows: "He has acquired the ability to see in himself what others fail to see!"

KEY Point To Remember: Egotistical bosses worry about the perception their managers and colleagues have of them. Give the ego-drive boss ideas he can proclaim and promulgate as his own. Let him run with your idea. So you don't get the credit you deserve. No big deal because you have the satisfaction of knowing it is your idea that is worthy enough for your boss to capitalize on. Remember: you look good when you help your boos look good.

Benevolent Dictator – This is the type of person who will give you the shirt off his back while stabbing you in the back. Hard working and courageous, this type of boss possesses a well-intended heart, but suffers from the super-controller syndrome. This boss micromanages everything. He receives a sense of power and satisfaction from controlling things and people. Like the *Super Ego*, he lives to find the smallest of error in the work of others.

He trusts you the way you'd trust a two-year old behind the wheel of your car. No matter how much detail you give this boss type, or how many times you redo a piece of work, it's never quite right. Working for a control freak leads people to put less energy into work in general and to invest their time and energy elsewhere. This type of boss also cripples the exchange of ideas and innovation. He fails to develop the leadership and initiative skills of his people. The good news about working for a benevolent dictator is that he wants you to succeed. The bad news is that he wants it done his way.

KEY Point To Remember: The bottom line with the Benevolent Dictator (BD) is to make sure you do great work and that he knows about it. You cannot survive with the BD by merely getting by. Perform well and befriend the BD and you will have a valuable career resource in your corner. If you fail to produce at a high level of competency, update your resume!

Napoleon Complex – This is one of my favorite types of ineffective managers because their behavior is so obvious to everyone except themselves. These are small men in stature and usually smaller yet in height who continually display their self-proclaimed manliness to prove their worth and maintain an illusion of "larger than life." These are the types of individuals who hang pictures in their office at lower than normal level to make themselves feel bigger!

As youths these little Napoleons never made the local Little League team because, in their minds, they were disadvantaged because of their size and the world was against them when in reality they just weren't any good at baseball. They carry that shortness burden into their working environment and turn out to be pains-in-the-rear for anyone around them. The Sabol rule when communicating face-to-face with these vertically challenged types: When you are in their presence, make them feel taller than they really are: remain seated!

While they can be an asset to an organization because they are normally bright and hard working, these individuals lack the interpersonal skills needed to bring out the best in others. These personality types reinforce the workplace axiom that job-seekers join great companies but leave because of bad bosses.

KEY Point To Remember: Two "do nots" to keep in mind: Do not underestimate the clout of the Napoleon type. He can be very influential within an organization because of intellect, drive, and personal relationships with higher-ups in the organization. Do not trust this individual to have your best interests in mind – especially if you are taller than he is.

Inherently Incompetent – Another bad boss type is the person who just doesn't have "it"....yet he does have the title and the authority to make your working life painful. "It" consists of the intellect, personal demeanor, and supervisory skills required to effectively manage. This person is not particularly bright, and adds to his deficiency by being a poor listener and narrow-minded.

This boss type survives because he surrounds himself with highly competent people. He is normally politically astute and knows who within his organization to support and who to avoid. He does not step outside of his comfort zone and avoids taking a risk at all costs. He has a keen ability to know what will make him look good. He will go to bat for you only on issues that serve his personal or political agenda. He's sneaky and plays favorites. He won't think twice about using you as a sacrificial lamb to support his own career goals.

Because he invests so much time in talking and in internal politics rather than in doing, he tends to promote people who are his friends rather than those who are most qualified for the position. Like the other three bad boss types, he can be extremely frustrating to work for.

KEY Point To Remember: If you are perceived to be a threat to his skills and competency, he is likely to discretely cut you off at the knees. He will promote others of lesser talent and drive because he does not see them as a threat to his domain. Support his high need for recognition by making him look good on strategic projects. Focus your own efforts on "high-value" work. Be prepared to share the limelight, even if it kills you.

No matter what type of bad boss you have to deal with, remember this: Learn from the experience. Very early on in my career, I worked for one of the worst bosses – out of a roster of many bad bosses – I had ever experienced. At our first staff meeting he informed those who reported to him that his job was to do absolutely nothing. And you know what? He excelled at his job. He did absolutely nothing. Over the years, I have used that experience with the do-nothing boss as an incentive to try and excel at my work. Put your bad boss experience to work for you.

How To Deal With Difficult Bosses

When dealing with these bosses remember that their irritating behavior is not personal. This is just they way these folks are. Here are methods for effectively coping with these bosses:

Remember: You have been successful before! – Remind yourself that you have been successful before you ever met this person.

Even if this is your first experience reporting to a difficult boss, you have been effective in many ways prior to your relationship with him or her. Think about projects and experiences you have had that were favorably recognized. These may have been in college or on a committee for a worthy cause. They may have happened before you joined your current employer or they may have been in a different area within your current employment. Remember that you are qualified for the job you have with or without the difficult boss – otherwise you would not likely be in the position you hold.

<u>Don't criticize your boss</u> – To get along with this boss, don't criticize him or her. Showing this person the errors of his ways is a death knell. Don't point out mistakes this person may have made. While she may benefit from your objective feedback, most bosses don't want to hear it. And be very careful with whom you speak about your boss. Don't assume that your friend and colleague at work will keep your comments private. Do not challenge your bosses' authority or his self-perceived greatness. Showing respect and even admiration for this bosses' accomplishments is not schmoozing; it is good common sense.

<u>Get it in writing</u> – Your position description is not enough. One means for increasing your effectiveness is to secure, whenever possible, written directions and expectations from your boss. This

will decrease the potential for uncertainty and you can use it discretely should you need to explain or to defend your actions. If you believe your boss will oppose written expectations, send an e-mail summarizing key issues that you and your boss discussed. This gesture can often eliminate misunderstanding while demonstrating your intention to meet your bosses' expectations.

Communicate privately – Another priority for coping with difficult bosses is to communicate face-to-face privately. Tell her what you need in direction, feedback, and support. Ask how you can help her reach her goals. Do your best to keep the boss in your communications. Above all, befriend her secretary. Secretaries are gatekeepers and vitally important to most bosses. Kind words from a secretary to her boss about an employee can go a long way to cultivating favorable relations with that boss.

Know your boss's business agenda – The business agenda, which may or may not have ever been communicated to staff members, is the overall goal your boss has for his function. This is not about strategic or department plans. This is about your boss's desire to achieve a specific overall organizational objective. What specifically does your boss want to achieve? Ask your boss what he wants to be remembered for when he leaves that organization. You need to know the answer to this question so you can help your boss achieve that goal.

Apply the magic wand – You need to know, early in your relationship, the expectations your boss has of you. Ask her this question: "If you had a magic wand and could create the ideal relationship between the two of us, what would that relationship be like?" Probe her. Ask her what has worked well in her relationships with staff in the past and what has not met her expectations. By seeking input directly from your boss early into your relationship you are demonstrating an interest in making the relationship work to the advantage of your boss and yourself.

Find a mentor – If you really like your employer, but really don't like your boss, another solution is to develop a mentoring relationship with a boss/supervisor in another part of the organization. Mentoring can be a great resource for acquiring valuable information from someone who "has been around the block a time or two" in the organization and perhaps has valuable insight from experience outside the organization. When coping with a bad boss, a mentor can be a good sounding board for you. If there is no mentor available within your current organization, seek one outside of the company.

Manage up – You are the one who must take responsibility for improving your relationship with a difficult boss. Keep in mind the value to manage up. Here are four action steps for managing up:

(1) *Train your boss to meet with you regularly.* This is not about monthly or weekly staff meetings. Meeting with your boss to discuss issues of importance to him or her will provide you with vital information for you to add value to your relationship with your boss.

(2) *Ask directly for constructive feedback, not just critical reaction, to your efforts.* While the onus shouldn't be on the individual to beg for praise, as an employee you can explain to your boss that such communication motivates you to deliver your very best work. The boss also benefits from the quality of your work. Ask for feedback on what you're doing right and where improvement on your part is needed.

(3) *Come to each meeting with an agenda.* Take notes on your agenda and retain it for future use. The mere fact that you are organized with an agenda and taking notes, is further evidence of your intent to meet the expectations of your boss. Better yet, this behavior may provide the fodder to exceed any expectations your boss has.

(4) *Anticipate problems and offer solutions.* One means to endear yourself to the difficult boss or to any boss is to not only think proactively, but to act proactively. I find it amazing how often well-paid professionals attend meetings and bring little, if anything of value, to the table. Endear yourself to your boss by bringing something to the table.

25 Ways To Score Base Hits and Even A Few Home Runs With Your Boss

1. ***Think Bottom Line*** – Senior management has its eye on the bottom line. With a bottom line mentality, you are able to focus on behavior that contributes to profitability and eliminate behavior that does not. Demonstrate that you understand bottom line thinking and execution.

2. ***Be Client/Customer Driven*** – Everyone who generates income has customers. Concern for clients is not just Marketing's responsibility. Determine how your job can be fine tuned to better serve the market your employer serves.

3. ***Attend Meetings Well Prepared*** – Read the agenda and all distributed reports and bring them with you to the

meeting. You are not scoring any hits with your boss by sitting in a meeting with nothing to contribute.

4. *Take Notes* – Unless you have a photographic memory, ask your boss if it is OK to take notes when you meet with him. You do not want to miss anything significant your boss discusses when you meet. Your attentiveness will score at least a single; maybe a double with your boss.

5. ***Do Not Bad Mouth Former Employer or Boss*** – No matter how negative your thoughts may be about your former employer or boss, never say anything negative about him in front of your current boss.

6. ***Ask Smart Questions*** – Four questions to occasionally ask your boss: (a) "Is there anything else I should know?" (b) "What do you think is the best way to proceed?" (c) "How do you envision the end result?" (d) "What would you do first?"

7. ***Do A Little Task*** – Taking the initiative to do a menial task shows your boss (and others) you are a no-nonsense person who can take charge. If you don't tackle an

occasional small task, why should your boss entrust you with a big task?

8. *Be Low Maintenance* – Learn to work with less supervision. Even bosses who are obsessive controllers, value their time. When in the middle of an assignment, take the initiative to do necessary research to come up with answers on your own.

9. ***Learn Which Of The Four Personality Styles Your Boss Possesses*** – Match your communications style with that of your boss. If your boss is either a *Controller* or a *Promoter*, get to the point sooner rather than later. If your boss is an *Analyzer,* speak more slowly and ask questions as you go along. For the *Supporter* boss, focus your attention on service and always follow-up with your commitments to him/her.

10. *Understand Your Boss's Motivation* – Is he or she looking for a promotion or recognition, or more money? What other factors could be driving your boss's work environment. Is there a sick spouse or child at home? A recent divorce or death? All could contribute to how your boss treats you!

11. *Think Big; Do Big; But Pay Attention to Details* – While it is important to envision the big picture – the overall goal of your organization – completing the details is what gets things done. Big projects get done by breaking them into smaller pieces. Stay focused on your day-to-day tasks.

12. *Learn From Your Mistakes* – Everyone makes mistakes. Those who rarely error are those who rarely risk. Every job-related adverse experience should be viewed as a learning opportunity. Learn from your mistakes so you do not repeat the same error in the future.

13. *Seek Self-Improvement* – Thomas Edison had very little formal education as a child, teaching himself much by reading on his own. This belief in self-improvement remained throughout his life. From college and university executive education to the Internet, the resources to learn at your computer are the most abundant in history. Take advantage of them to become more valuable to yourself and to your boss.

14. *Be Inquisitive* – Prescription without diagnosis puts medical professionals – and their patients – at risk. Asking questions is vital to understanding specifically

what your boss wants. Don't be shy about asking your boss questions before taking on an assignment.

15. *Never Argue With Your Boss* – It makes no difference if you are correct in the position you take. What can you possibly gain by winning the battle and losing the war – except ego gratification? Argumentativeness, a counterproductive behavior, is nothing more than fodder for a boss with a long memory...or a short one for that matter.

16. *Empathize With Your Boss* – When you put yourself in your boss's shoes you realize the true test of empathy. Speak or act as though you were about to hear or experience what you would say or do. Imagine yourself sitting at your boss's desk trying to make decisions. Your perspective will change quickly.

17. *Accept Criticism Positively* – A boss's criticism is rarely, if ever, personal. In *The Godfather,* Consiliari Tom Hagen exclaims: "Even the shooting of your father was business, not personal, Sonny!" Avoid responding in anger or acting defensively. Accept criticism and respond to your boss by saying something similar to the following: "Thank you for calling this to my attention. I will do my

best to improve my work." This will go a long way toward instilling a mature, professional impression upon your boss.

18. *Do Not Complain – Do Offer Solutions* – When you go to your boss to complain about something or some person, there's a good chance she already knows about it. No one enjoys listening to a person complain about what's wrong but never has solutions. No one wants another problem, but bosses do want solutions.

19. *Secure Performance Reviews* – Two of the biggest mistakes bosses continue to make are the avoidance of providing employees with regular performance reviews and for those who do provide reviews, conducting them only every 12 months. Don't wait for your boss to provide you with an annual review – it may be too late to correct shortcomings in your performance. Meet with your boss at least semi-annually to examine your technical performance and your personal relationships skills. Take the feedback to heart.

20. *Be An Expert At Listening* – Knowledge speaks; wisdom listens! Listening well signals respect for your boss and that you have exemplary business decorum. Hold off on

presenting your agenda until the other person has finished his statement.

21. ***Befriend Your Boss's Secretary*** – Your boss's secretary is a primary gatekeeper to your boss. Do not underestimate the influence of his/her opinion. She has your boss's ear. She is in a position to influence your boss's impression of you.

22. ***Apply The Magic Wand*** – Knowing exactly what is required of you in terms of your relationship with your boss beyond your position description is vital. Ask your boss if she had a magic wand and could create the ideal relationship with you at work, what would that relationship be like.

23. ***Maintain A Sense Of Humor*** – Lighten up! A sense of humor helps keep work and life in proper perspective. Match your sense of humor with what is appreciated by your boss.

24. ***Bring Enthusiasm To Your Job*** – If you are not enthused about your job, your boss and others will know. Victor Frankl, Holocaust survivor and internationally respected philosopher and writer, said: *"Everything can be taken*

from a man but …the last of the human freedoms - to choose one's attitude in any given set of circumstances, to choose one's own way." Our enthusiasm drives our behavior. Bring enthusiasm to your work or find your enthusiasm elsewhere!

25. *Understand Three Kinds Of People* – There are three kinds of people in business: Those who make things happen; those who watch things happen; and those who wondered what happened. Taking charge and showing initiative is a sign of leadership. When you make things happen, rather than sitting back and waiting to see what happens, you endear yourself to your boss. Remember: "Doing nothing is very hard to do…you never know when you are finished!"

Chapter 9 – Coping With The Difficult Co-Worker

> *"You don't mind getting on people's nerves, do you?*
> Attorney Douglas Caddy
> *All The President's Men* (1976)

Difficult encounters at work are not limited to those with your boss. Enter the difficult and challenging co-worker. This is the person who *r e a l l y* bugs you. Until now, you thought your boss was a bit difficult. How about the co-worker who brings so much baggage with him to work that he needs a backpack to carry it all! Chances are that you have had to deal with such a person. You may be dealing with this type of person right now.

Learning to cope with difficult co-workers is essential for succeeding at work. Nearly every organization comes staffed with at least one individual who is unpleasant – or even hostile. Knowing how to deal effectively with this challenging personality can benefit your work life and your life away from your job as well.

Annoying and damaging co-worker actions can range from extremely passive to obnoxious to aggressive to bullying. Aggression and bullying are not necessarily the same. Whereas aggression may involve a single act, bullying involves repeated attacks against a target creating an on-going pattern of behavior according to the Safety & Health Assessment and Research for Prevention (SHARP), an independent research program within the Washington State Department of Labor and Industries. "Tough" or "demanding" bosses are not necessarily bullies, as long as their primary motivation is to obtain the best performance by setting high expectations according SHARP (Report # 87-1-2006).

Workplace bullying is an emerging concern for United States organizations according to research by the National Institute for Occupational Safety and Health (NIOSH). One in four companies has experienced workplace bullying, and most incidents of bullying appear to be done by employees against one another NIOSH reports. For this study, bullying was defined as repeated intimidation, slandering, social isolation, or humiliation by one or more persons against another. This type of aggressive behavior is not limited to any one type of co-worker. It seems that all types join in on the activity.

In the U.S. workplace, it has been shown that psychological aggression is a pervasive issue. Loraleigh Keashly and Karen Jagatic reported in *The Nature, Extent, and Impact of Emotional Abuse in the Workplace* results of a statewide survey that 50 percent of the representative sample of a statewide survey in Michigan said that they had experienced at least one type of emotional abuse at the hands of co-workers, and that 27 percent reported being mistreated by a co-worker in the past twelve months.

The cost of this type of behavior can be substantial. According to NIOSH research, workplace bullying has been shown to impact the individual, with some research finding increased symptoms of depression, anxiety, and psychosomatic complaints in those who are victimized and sometimes in those who were not victims themselves but were witnesses present in the work environment. NIOSH further reported that bullying has been associated with absenteeism, higher turnover rate, reduced productivity, and litigation costs.

In addition, bullies do not run good organizations according to SHARP. Staff turnover and sick leave will be high, while morale and productivity will be low. Stress, depression, and physical health problems result in time away from work that is costly in terms of workers' compensation and lost productivity. Exhibit 9 at the end of this chapter lists sources of valuable information on bullying in the workplace.

The trust that employees normally enjoy in a favorable work environment gets lost in a bullying environment. This breakdown in trust contributes to the failure of employees to do their best work. They do not give extra effort that could be crucial to an organization's success. These employees are more inclined to hold back on providing ideas for improvement and they may be less honest about performance. No one wins in these types of work environments. Change must take place. You are the change master.

> *"They always say that time changes things, but you actually have to change them yourself."*
> Andy Warhol

When you sense a problem is on the horizon, determine if you have to solve the problem with your co-worker or if you can tolerate it. Give your co-worker the benefit of the doubt. He may not even know that he is a pain to be around, especially if no one else has done anything to create a change for the better. If this person's behavior is limited to just annoying you, tolerating the person may be the choice to make. On the other hand, if this person interferes with your ability to perform your function at work, you need to find a way to resolve this problem. Focusing your attention on the following action steps will help produce an improved relationship with that difficult person.

- *The first thing to do is an action not to take.*

Do not contact your boss to discuss the problem you are having with the difficult person. Bosses normally expect employees to work out problems amongst themselves at their level. Don't forget: for all you know your boss may think the other person is just fine. Your boss and the other person may be old family friends. For a variety of reasons, do not – at this point – seek counsel from your boss.

• *Discuss the situation with a trusted friend or colleague.*

If you have a colleague who works with this person and tends to get along with him or her, find out what your friend does to make their relationship work. Go to your mentor and seek advice. If you don't have a mentor, find one. Discuss – don't complain – face-to-face specific issues that you believe need to be addressed with the difficult person. Communicate with this friend that you realize in any relationship, both parties influence the other's behavior. Focusing on blame may give you temporary reprieve, but it will serve no constructive purpose. Your primary objective in this discussion is to obtain objective opinion on what needs to be done to improve your relationship with the difficult person.

• *Communicate face-to-face privately with the difficult co-worker.*

Bring up the problem directly and privately with your co-worker. Your relations with him may suffer if he finds out about the problem first from someone else. By bringing up the problem directly, you are sending a message that you have confidence that both of you can resolve differences.

Approach the person in a polite, non-threatening manner. When contacting the difficult person, keep in mind that you may have contributed to the problems you are having with the other person. You may have a few idiosyncrasies that have drawn the attention of others. Be aware that the other person may not know just how irritating you find him. Talk with him about what you are experiencing. Do not accuse the other person. As challenging as it may be, always remain calm. Keep your cool. Do not meet with this person if you are tense, mad, or upset in any way. You might say something like this:

> *"Mark I appreciate your finding time to meet. I've noticed that you and I have some differences and I thought it best for the two of us to discuss them. I have some thoughts on how we might be able to work together more effectively, but I would really like to know your thoughts on what I might do to help our relationship. Is there anything I can do to make things better between the two of us?"*

Your main goal is to create an open dialog with the other person. Listen intently to what he says and the manner in which he says it. By demonstrating acute listening, you are reinforcing the value you place on his feedback. Remember that there should always be a "next step" – some type of action to be taken – produced during this meeting. Do not get caught in the "let me

CHAPTER 9 – Coping With The Difficult Co-Worker   131

think about it" syndrome. Follow through with any agreed upon action.

• *Follow-up.*

After a reasonable length of time, follow up with the other person by asking if he or she has observed the agreed-upon action you were to take. Has the difficult co-worker's behavior changed for the better or not at all? If it has not changed – some co-workers just don't give a damn about other's feeling and concerns – determine if you want to confront this person again by yourself.

• *Take the group approach.*

If the other person is not responding to your liking, you have a couple of considerations. You can ignore him and hope that some miraculous cure will present itself…not a likely scenario. You can go over the person's head and talk to his boss…not recommended just yet. You can take the group approach…a better choice at the moment. If others are as frustrated with the other person as you are, talk with them and set a meeting to discuss face-to-face issues with the difficult co-worker. Sometimes, when the difficult person is faced with several disgruntled co-workers, all in unison expressing their displeasure, behavior change can occur for the better.

- *Limit access to you.*

If your work requirements allow, separate yourself from the co-worker. Avoid being on the same committees. Seek opportunities within your organization that do not include this person.

I met with one of the two co-managing partners of a professional service firm in San Francisco. Both partners were responsible for the strategic direction and financial success of that office. Nothing unique about that, right? How's this: They couldn't stand each other. In fact, they never talked to each other. That is not an enjoyable atmosphere when you spend eight or nine hours a day. This is a classic example of neither person creating change for the better.

- *Get the boss involved.*

When the above-referenced avenues to resolve issues with the difficult co-worker have been exhausted, seek input from your boss on how to deal with this issue. Those who supervise and manage others are responsible for applying management skills that are in the best interests of their employer and employees. Now is the time for the boss to manage.

In a cool, calm, and collected manner inform your boss of the continued unacceptable behavior of the co-worker, and the steps you have taken to resolve differences with that person. While there is a certain risk when contacting your boss, your choices for resolution, at this point, are limited. You are, therefore, not only justified in communicating with your boss regarding the issue at hand, but also you have a responsibility to your employer and to your career to do what you can to make things better.

• *Try a thank-you.*

If you have a sense that the co-worker has changed or is making a concerted effort to change for the better, acknowledge that person's effort. Thank her, even if her efforts have not been 100 percent successful. The mere fact that you acknowledge her actions to correct this behavior may reinforce her willingness to continue to do so. Who knows, she may end up working for you some day, and wouldn't it be gratifying to know that you helped turn her into a colleague.

Exhibit 9

References:

The following website/organizations have put together valuable information that includes definitions and facts about bullying in the workplace:

UK National Workplace Bullying Alliance Line
(http://www.bullyingonlinelorg/workbully/bully.htm)
European Agency for Safety and Health at Work Facts: Bullying at Work
(http://agency.osha.eu.int/publications/factsheets/23/factsheetsn23_en.pdf)
The Commission of Occupational Safety and Health
(http://www.worksafe.wa.gov.au/newsite/worksafe/media/Guide_bullying_employ.pdf)

NIOSH Update: Most Workplace Bullying is Worker to Worker
(http://www.cdc.gov/niosh/updates/upd-07-28-04.htm)
Workplace Bullying and Trauma Institute, Bellingham, Washington (http://www.bullyinginstitute.org/)

Guide for Employers on Workplace Bullying
(http://www.worksafe.wa.gov.au/newsite/worksafe/meida/Guide_bullying_emplo.pdf)
Guide for Employees on Workplace Bullying
(http://www.workshafe.wa.gov.au/newsite/worksafe/media/Guide_bulying_emplo.pdf)

Research References:

Glendinnig, P. M. (2001). Workplace bullying: Curing the cancer of the American workplace. *Public Personnel Management*, Vol. 30, pp. 269-285.

Spector, P. E. & Fox, S. (2005). Stressor-emotion model. In S. Fox and P. E. Spector (Eds.) Counterproductive Work Behavior: Investigations of Actors and Targets (pp.151-174), American Psychological Association: Washington, DC.

Keashly, L. & Harvey, S. (2005). Emotional Abuse in the Workplace. In S. Fox and P.E. Spector (Eds.) *Counterproductive Work Behavior: Investigations of Actors and Targets* (pp.301-235), American Psychological Association: Washington, DC.

Raynor, C. & Keashly, L. (2005). Bullying at work: A perspective from Britain and North America. In S. Fox and P. E. Spector (Eds.) *Counterproductive Work Behavior: Investigations of Actors and Targets* (pp.271-296), American Psychological Association: Washington, DC.

Salin, D. (2003). Way of explaining workplace bullying: A review of enabling, motivating, and precipitating structures and processes in the work environment. *Human Relations*, Vol. 56, pp. 1213-1232.

Chapter 10 – Coping With The Super Aggressive

> *"Never hate your enemies, it affects your judgement."*
> Michael Corleone
> *The Godfather* (1972)

These folks come in a variety of packages and can make your work life very difficult. They may be your immediate superior. They may be the chair of a committee the both of you are on; they may be a colleague you just happened to get stuck with because the two of you were hired the same week and your last names begin with the same first letter. These people seem to be on a mission that can result in self-destruction or a mission that unjustifiably harms others. They can be intimidating, highly critical and are normally supported by an oversized arrogance.

Aggressive behavior is behavior that unjustifiably harms another. According to Roy H. Lubit, author of *Coping with Toxic Managers,* aggression is driven both by frustrations that are inherent in working in organizations and by competition to advance one's personal and work agenda. "Most people experience these feelings. Most of us are aggressive at times. Not everyone, however, acts on these feelings in ways that are markedly unfair and hurt others," says Lubit. "Some people seem to have an unusual talent for stepping on those around them. An individual's personality traits, moral beliefs, and the culture in which she works and lives have tremendous impact on how aggressively she acts at work."

Behavior that may initially appear to be aggressive may, indeed, be nothing more than assertive behavior. There is a difference between the two worth noting. Fellow workers are entitled to be assertive. Workers are not entitled to be super aggressive. Where assertiveness entails making clear statements of what a person wants – even though they may not be statements another person wants to hear – super aggressiveness includes destructive behavior. Informing a co-worker that you expect from him specific action and telling him the consequences if he fails to comply with your request is being assertive. It is not being super aggressive.

Insulting a fellow worker or making disparaging remarks to this person goes beyond being assertive and quickly forms highly aggressive behavior. Damaging another's reputation because she did not support an initiative important to you, is super aggressive.

Super aggressives love to use questions as a way to place the other person on the defense. They attempt to gain the upper hand quickly in their effort to control the other person. The aggressive person enjoys using these expressions to maintain control in his communications:

CHAPTER 10 – Coping With The Super Aggressive

Why did you............
Why didn't you............
What was the reason for............
Why would you............
What were you thinking when you............

> *"When I get ready to reason with a man, I spend one-third of my time thinking about myself and what I am going to say - - and two-thirds thinking about him and what he is going to say."*
> Abraham Lincoln

Don't get caught off guard by the aggressive person's love fest with questions. Anticipate that you will be on the receiving end of a series of questions during certain encounters with the supper aggressive. Anticipate questions that may be thrown at you and think of responses in advance of your encounter. You will not only neutralize the aggressive person's behavior, you will reduce his tendencies to place you on the defensive in the future.

The following are action steps you can take to counter the aggressive individual:

<u>Maintain your composure</u> – First of all: Keep your cool. Your goal is to speak assertively, not aggressively and to calmly persevere. If you are extremely angry with this person, you risk

escalating the conflict when you respond in an emotional state. Do not confront someone when you are angry or frustrated. Take time to relax as best you can. In addition to clouding your thinking and your responding to the other person when you are emotional, you look bad in front of others. Remember, you are a professional. In spite of the other person's attitude, you maintain control.

<u>Use the person's name with distinction</u> – You want to remain in control during this encounter. By using the person's name in the same manner you normally do, you are helping to maintain control of your emotions. If you normally address him as Mr. Smith, use that same format. If you normally use his first name, follow that procedure.

<u>Stand up to this person</u> – You have more than a right – you have a personal responsibility – to counter the statements of the super-aggressive. Aggressive people require assertive responses. "Your behavior must send a clear message that you are strong and capable, since anything less is an invitation for further attacks," according to Dr. Rick Brinkman and Dr. Rick Kirschner in their book, *Dealing <u>With</u> People You Can't Stand*. You are not seeking a confrontation. You are seeking respect. If you are in a face-to-face encounter, stand up. Try not to remain seated. Do not leap to your feet; rather carry yourself in a dignified, but firm standing

CHAPTER 10 – Coping With The Super Aggressive

posture. Individuals who stand over another person assume a position of authority. By standing facing the aggressive individual you are neutralizing his physical positioning.

<u>Acknowledge body language</u> – The most important message is the message received. Despite what we may intend to say with our words, our body language is often the over-riding factor in how the message is received. By being tuned into the body posture of the difficult person, you will increase your chances of understanding the real meaning of what he or she is saying. Police departments spend hours training their officers on ways to detect various specific non-vocal messages. For example, lies can be detected by pupil size; the fact that someone is holding back information can be detected by a 'guarded' posture (arms folded). Small libraries exist on the subject of body language. The more knowledgeable you are of how body language influences communications, the better equipped you will be to deal effectively with this type of person.

If you are inclined to expand your knowledge of how body language and related behavior influence communicating and relating to another person, you would do well to access the writings of Dr. Michael Brooks on using NeuroLinguistic Programming (NLP). As Brooks points out in *The Power of Business Rapport*, "NLP, as model of behavior that allows us to achieve immediate connection and thus influence others, is the invisible catalyst that brings people together by maximizing commonality and minimizing disparity." Another quality source for NLP knowledge is the writings of Steve Andreas and Charles Faulker.

Get the person to sit down – People are normally more calm when they are seated as opposed to when they can stand and move about. Spatial changes give a tone to a communication, accent it, and at times even counteract the spoken word. A person who enters an office and stands as opposed to being seated gains dominant body language that can influence the conversation on a subconscious level.

Maintain proper space – Behavioral studies indicate that individuals perceive a distance – their personal space – that is appropriate for different types of messages. Research supports the hypothesis that the violation of this personal space can have serious adverse effects on communication. Respect the other person's space by maintaining reasonable distance between that person and yourself.

Avoid a fight – You can win the fight with the difficult person, but end up losing the war. Gaining the upper hand in a heated discussion with the super-aggressive personality may prove of little long-range value. You may do more damage to your reputation and to your career when winning a confrontation. No one is suggesting that you let the other person run over you. The recommended solution is to avoid the fight and the war by outsmarting your opponent. As American writer James Thurber stated the issue so well: "Let us not look back in anger or forward in fear, but around in awareness." Use your superior emotional control, intellect, and communications skills to prove that you are in command of your own destiny.

Chapter 11 – Coping With The Silent Type

> *"Stop trying to rationalize everything, will ya? Let's face it, we have a mystery on our hands."*
> Jack Belicec
> *Invasion of The Body Snatchers* (1956)

Some might think that silence as a form of aggression is an oxymoron. Not so. Aggression is not limited to ranting, raving or bullying. When you need information from someone and that person does what he can to make certain you don't get it when you need it, that behavior is one of aggression. That person is exercising a form of control: "I have what you need and you're not getting it from me when you need it." And the *Silent Type* can pop up just about anywhere.

Soils was the name of this guy in my Army basic training platoon at Fort Polk, Louisiana. He stood about 6'4'' and weighed a solid 230. Soils was the kind of guy you would want along side of you when walking through a dark alley. He had a scar that started above his left eye and ended somewhere around the lower right side of his chin. I didn't ask him how he got the scar; I didn't want to know. Soils was big, strong, and chiseled, but that's not what made him unique. What made him unique was that he said very little to anyone. When our drill instructor gave orders to do push-ups, Soils took the prone position as if to start doing push-ups with the rest of us, but he never did his push-ups. When our DI yelled at him to do push-ups, Soils responded in two ways: He didn't do push-ups and he never said a word. The more our DI tried to get him to do his push-ups, and the more frustrated our DI got, Soils said nothing. Soils was in control. He was able to do just what he wanted to do, which was to be in control of his immediate environment.

How do I know Soils was as strong as he looked and probably capable of doing push-ups on one finger? Fast forward to the pugil stick competition. This is where you don some protective gear and blast away with padded oars in an attempt to beat the stuffing out of your opponent. It was now time for the Company pugil stick championship. The two finalists in each platoon would fight each other to determine the platoon champion who would then go on to fight in the Company competition. I won all of my fights and was then awarded the opportunity to slug it out for the platoon championship with the other finalist. Now just who do you think I was matched with? Where was Woody Allen when I needed him? My opponent was, of course, Soils. He had not just won his fights, Soils sent half of his opponents to the infirmary for body part replacements! Our DI rewarded me by having the two of us fight not once, but the best of two out of three. Just what I wanted. If King Kong had an understudy, I was about to face him. Soils won the first fight. I won the second. After an intensive third go-round, the epic battle was declared a draw. The DI flipped a coin to see who would represent our platoon in the Company competition. If I had a rosary with me at the time I would have broken it out and cranked on a few beads hoping that Soils would get the nod. As it turned out I didn't need my rosary – my prayers were answered. Soils won the toss and proceeded to annihilate the other platoon champions. All along, Soils, who said very little, was in control. Even pugil stick champions can control their environment and get what they want through silence.

> *"Lying is done with words and also with silence."*
> Adrienne Rich

Not all of the silent type's behavior is always so obvious. Here are characteristics of the silent type:

- Does not state thoughts and feelings truly and directly
- Does not meet deadlines
- Does not respond on time
- Wants you to think he or she will comply by due date and on time
- Is apologetic
- Gives in to requests and demands of others

- Allows others to make decisions for him or her
- Discounts his or her own worth
- Allows others to take advantage of him or her

In addition to those who exercise control by applying the above behavior, there are those who honestly feel they have nothing to contribute in a group meeting or similar exchange. They may be insecure; they may be intimidated. Regardless of their reasons for going quiet, they remain a roadblock to what you need. Your goal is to diplomatically get them to open up. When they are silent and you have a need from them, they are in control. Here are some action steps to get them to communicate and for you to regain control:

<u>Ask open-ended questions</u>. The last thing you want to solicit is a "yes" or a "no". Include in your questioning: *Who, what, when, where,* and *how*. These words seek a request for specific information, making it difficult for the silent type to remain silent. Keep in mind that when asking open-ended questions of the silent type, you may have to practice your own silence, remembering that *silence is golden*. Wait patiently, maintaining eye contact and proper behavioral space, for the person to respond. If you know this silent person falls into the Analyzer quadrant, you know he or she will likely process information

more slowly. Give them ample time to think and to open up and give you the information you seek.

Here are a few questions you can use to stimulate the reaction you want from that silent person:

> *"What is your reaction so far to what we have discussed?"*
>
> *"What are some of your thoughts on what we have talked about?"*
>
> *"What do you think the next step might be?"*
>
> *"Where shall we go from here?"*
>
> *"How do you want to proceed?"*

Comment on what is happening (or what is not happening).

Sample questions:

> *"John. I expected you to say something, and you're not. What does that mean?"*
>
> *"Ruth, this is in your specialty area and you seem reluctant to speak up. Please tell me why you are not giving us your opinion on this?"*

Apply group/team pressure:
Sample questions:

> *"We have a great opportunity to exceed our goal and no one's input is more important than Bob's. What do you think our group will need, Bob, to hit that target?"*
>
> *"In what direction do you think our team should go, Judy, if we are to make our unit's deadline?"*

If the silent person fails to respond, he remains in control. You still don't have the information you need. Now is the time for Plan B: Get creative. If he responds to one of your open-ended questions with "I really don't know" or "I'm not sure", place the onus back on him: "Guess!" or you might say, "If you did know, what do you think it might be?" or "You're creative. Take your best shot. What do think might happen next?"

Remember to place yourself as best you can in the silent type's shoes. Think of why you believe he or she is that way. What is their motivation for clamming up? If you were that person, what form of communications would motivate you to respond? As you determine those motivating factors, selectively apply them to remove the shackles surrounding the silent type and to secure control of the communications you desire.

Chapter 12 – You Are The Solution

> *"Over, did you say 'over'. Nothing is over until we say it is. Was it over when the Germans bombed Pearl Harbor?"*
> John 'Bluto' Blutarsky
> *Animal House* (1978)

You have a variety of choices in how you communicate and deal with the difficult person. You can do nothing and hope things will get better. You can anticipate that the difficult and challenging personality will see weakness in his ways and will seek a means to amend his attitude and behavior. My advice: don't count on it! You cannot rely on the person you find challenging and difficult to create change for the better. If that were the case, you would probably not be reading this book. Why would they change their attitude or their behavior if their communications and actions have for years gone unchecked or have continually been ignored? Difficult people are not motivated to make your life easier and your career more enjoyable.

You have to take the lead to make things better. You are the remedy for what ails your relations with the problem person.

No one but you is going to make the irritants of communicating and coping with the challenging person go away.

> *"If it is to be....it's up to me."*
> Anonymous

Dealing effectively with challenging personalities will mean being aware of those things people say or do that set us off on an emotional rollercoaster. In *Resolving Conflict*, authors Kenneth Cloke and Joan Goldsmith point out the need to recognize our hot buttons. "When we are able to identify the specific behaviors that push our buttons and speak honestly and vulnerably about them, we can often defuse them and become less emotionally reactive when someone pushes them."

Communicating with the difficult person means we may be on the receiving end of criticism. When you open the doors for dialogue with a challenging personality, he may welcome the opportunity to air out his feelings about relationship issues. Constructive criticism – not aggressive diatribes – of oneself can be a blessing in disguise. The fact that you are being criticized may well be an indication of high expectations others have of you. Consider the alternative: Never receiving constructive criticism could mean no one really cares what you do or what you think – not a favorable career path to be on.

When criticism is presented in the best of intentions, strong people learn and grow from the experience. They do not get defensive. They listen intently to what is being said. By acknowledging constructive criticism, you release any need to defend or to justify your position. You simply hear what the other person has to say. Whether you agree or you disagree with what is presented is irrelevant to your need to be open and mindful of the input. Your initial objective, when receiving constructive criticism, is to absorb what is being said and to express appreciation for the input. You should feel comfortable saying something like:

> *"I appreciate your taking time to let me know how you feel."*
> *"Your opinion is important to me. Thank you for sharing your thoughts with me."*

Dealing with the difficult person – boss or co-worker – may lead you to think of yourself as a victim. You're not. As mentioned earlier, the behavior of the difficult person is seldom, if ever, personal. As Eleanor Roosevelt so prominently said, "You're nobody's victim without your permission." No one controls your thoughts but you. No one controls you unless you allow it. By taking control of your workplace experience you are no longer the victim of difficult experiences. When you embrace the following behavior, you take control of your daily work life:

You are your own security – No one but you is responsible for your career. You are in charge of your future. Think of yourself as the CEO of your work life. When you look in the mirror you are seeing your very own CEO. Always perform to your highest potential and market yourself internally and externally. The better known you are within your organization, the easier it is to acquire any needed support when dealing with difficult co-workers. The better known you are outside of your employer, the easier it is to make a career transition should you choose to do so.

Take ownership in the quality of your work relationships – When you take the initiative and create change for the better with challenging personalities, great things can happen. You set a positive example for others to follow who may have challenges similar to yours. You create a more harmonious atmosphere for yourself and for co-workers. Anne Frank captured the essence of this issue when she said: "How wonderful it is that nobody need wait a single moment before starting to improve the world."

While changing the world may not be your goal in life, you can take pride knowing that through your ability to communicate and deal effectively with challenging personalities, your life at work and at home will be all the more enjoyable.

NOTES

Chapter 2

Page 13 – Kaiser Family Foundation Employer Health Benefits 2006 Annual Survey [www.kff.org/insurance/7527/upload/7578.pdf.] (February 2007)

Page 14 – Daniel Dana, Ph.D., *Managing Differences*, Fourth Edition, MTI Publications, July 2006

Page 17 – Survey: Elevated Stress Levels Lead to 'Presenteeism' [http://comp.blr.com/display.cfm?id=151399] (February 2007)

Page 20 - *Duxbury & Higgins, Work-Life Conflict in Canada in the New Millenium: A Status Report, 2003.*

Page 20 - *WarrenShepel [online] Health & Wellness Research Database, 2005*

Chapter 3

Page 28 – Roy H. Lubit, M.D., Ph.D. *Coping With Toxic Managers, Subordinates and other difficult people,* Prentice Hall, 2004

Chapter 5

Page 47 – Dr. Lyman K. Steil and Dr. Richard K. Bommelje, *Listening Leaders*, Beavers Pond Press, Inc., June 2004

Page 67 - [http://www.brainyquote.com/quotes/quotes/l/leeiacocca149253.html] (February 2007)

Page 80 – Dr. Michael Brooks, *Instant Rapport*, Warner Books, 1989

Page 83 – Dr. Rick Brinkman and Dr. Rick Kirschner, *Dealing with People You Can't Stand*, McGraw-Hill, 2002

Page 84 – Stephen R. Covey, *The 7 Habits of Highly Effective People*, Simon & Schuster, 1990

Chapter 8

Page 97 – Gallup Poll source – [http://www.fabjob.com/tips6.html], (March 2007)

Page 100 - *Primal Leadership:* Goleman, Daniel, Boyatzis, Richard, and McKay, Annie (Harvard Business School Press, 20002)

Chapter 9

Page 126 - Keasly, L & Jagatic, K (2000). The nature and extent of emotional abuse at work: Results of a statewide survey. Paper presented at the symposium on persistent patterns of aggressive behavior at work, Academy of Management annual Meeting, August, Toronto.

Page 128 –Andy Warhol, [http://www.brainyquote.com/quotes/ Authors/andy_warhol.html] (March 2007)

Page 133 - Exhibit 9 Source: Safety & Health Assessment and Research for Prevention (SHARP) Report # 87-1-2006. August 2006.

Chapter 10

Page 139 - Dr. Michael Brooks, *The Power of Business Rapport*, Harper Collins *Publishers,* 1991

Chapter 12

Page 150 – Kenneth Cole and Joan Goldsmith, *Resolving Conflicts At Work (Revised Edition),* Jossey-Bass, 2005